The

DICTIONARY *of*
OBSCURE SORROWS

JOHN KOENIG

SIMON & SCHUSTER

NEW YORK   LONDON   TORONTO   SYDNEY   NEW DELHI

Simon & Schuster
1230 Avenue of the Americas
New York, NY 10020

First Simon & Schuster hardcover edition November 2021

SIMON & SCHUSTER and colophon are registered trademarks of Simon & Schuster, Inc.

For information about special discounts for bulk purchases, please contact Simon & Schuster Special Sales at 1-866-506-1949 or business@simonandschuster.com.

The Simon & Schuster Speakers Bureau can bring authors to your live event. For more information or to book an event, contact the Simon & Schuster Speakers Bureau at 1-866-248-3049 or visit our website at www.simonspeakers.com.

Interior design by Carly Loman

Manufactured in the United States of America

10   9   8

Library of Congress Cataloging-in-Publication Data has been applied for.

ISBN 978-1-5011-5364-8
ISBN 978-1-5011-5366-2 (ebook)

CONTENTS

I read the dictionary.
I thought it was a poem
about everything.

—STEVEN WRIGHT

ABOUT THIS BOOK

The Dictionary of Obscure Sorrows is a compendium of new words for emotions. Its mission is to shine a light on the fundamental strangeness of being a human being—all the aches, demons, vibes, joys, and urges that are humming in the background of everyday life:

kenopsia: the atmosphere of a place that is usually bustling with people but is now abandoned and quiet.

dès vu: the awareness that this moment will become a memory.

nodus tollens: the feeling that the plot of your life doesn't make sense to you anymore.

énouement: the bittersweetness of having arrived here in the future, seeing how things turn out, but unable to tell your past self.

onism: the frustration of being stuck in just one body, that inhabits only one place at a time.

sonder: the realization that each random passerby is the main character of their own story, in which you are just an extra in the background.

It's a calming thing, to learn there's a word for something you've felt all your life but didn't know was shared by anyone else. It's even oddly empowering—to be reminded that you're not alone, you're not crazy, you're just an ordinary human being trying to make your way through a bizarre set of circumstances.

That's how the idea for this book was born, in that jolt of recognition you feel when learning certain words for emotions, especially in languages other than English: *hygge*, *saudade*, *duende*, *ubuntu*, *schadenfreude*. Some of these terms might well be untranslatable, but they still have the power to make the inside of your head feel a little more familiar, at least for a moment or two. It makes you wonder what else might be possible—what other morsels of meaning could've been teased out of the static, if only someone had come along and given them a name.

Of course, we don't usually question why a language has words for some things and not others. We don't really imagine we have much choice in the matter, because the words we use to build our lives were mostly handed to us in the crib or picked up on the playground. They function as a kind of psychological programming that helps shape our relationships, our memory, even our perception of reality.

As Wittgenstein wrote, "The limits of my language are the limits of my world."

But therein lies a problem. Language is so fundamental to our perception, we're unable to perceive the flaws built into language itself. It would be difficult to tell, for example, if our vocabulary had fallen badly out of date, and no longer described the world in which we live. We would feel only a strange hollowness in our conversations, never really sure if we're being understood.

The dictionary evolves over time, of course. New words are coined as needed, emerging one by one from the test lab of our conversations. But that process carries a certain bias, only giving names to concepts that are simple, tangible, communal, and easy to talk about.

Emotions are none of these. As a result, there's a huge blind spot in the language of emotion, vast holes in the lexicon that we don't even know we're missing. We have thousands of words for different types of finches and schooners and historical undergarments, but only a rudimentary vocabulary to capture the delectable subtleties of the human experience.

Words will never do us justice. But we have to try anyway. Luckily, the palette of language is infinitely expandable. If we wanted to, we could build a new linguistic framework to fill in the gaps, this time rooted in our common humanity, our shared vulnerability, and our complexity as individuals—a perspective that simply wasn't there when most of our dictionaries were written. We could catalog even the faintest quirks of the human condition, even things that were only ever felt by one person—though it is the working hypothesis of this book that none of us is truly alone in how we feel.

In language, all things are possible. Which means that no emotion is untranslatable. No sorrow is too obscure to define. We just have to do it.

This is not a book about sadness—at least, not in the modern sense of the word. The word *sadness* originally meant "fullness," from the same Latin root, *satis*, that also gave us *sated* and *satisfaction*. Not so long ago, to be sad meant you were filled to the brim with some intensity of experience. It wasn't just a malfunction in the joy machine. It was a state of awareness—setting the focus to infinity and taking it all in, joy and grief all at once. When we speak of sadness these days, most of the time what we really mean is despair, which is literally defined as the absence of hope. But true sadness is actually the opposite, an exuberant upwelling that reminds you how fleeting and mysterious and open-ended life can be. That's why you'll find traces of the blues all over this book, but you might find yourself feeling strangely joyful at the end of it. And if you are lucky enough to feel sad, well, savor it while it lasts—if only because it means that you care about something in this world enough to let it under your skin.

This is a dictionary—a poem about everything. It's divided into six chapters, with definitions grouped according to theme: the outer world, the inner self, the people you know, the people you don't, the passage of time, and the search for meaning. The definitions are arranged in no particular order, which seems fairly true to life, given the way emotions tend to drift through your mind like the weather.

All words in this dictionary are new. Some were rescued from the trash heap and redefined, others were invented from whole cloth, but most were stitched together from fragments of a hundred different languages, both living and dead. These words were not necessarily intended to be used in conversation, but to exist for their own sake. To give some semblance of order to the wilderness inside your head, so you can settle it yourself on your own terms, without feeling too lost—safe in the knowledge that we're all lost.

ONE

Between Living and Dreaming

SEEING THE WORLD AS IT IS,
AND THE WORLD AS IT COULD BE

Collage by Bruno Baraldi | TAKI

The bright side of the planet moves toward darkness
And the cities are falling asleep, each in its hour,
And for me, now as then, it is too much,
There is too much world.

—CZESŁAW MIŁOSZ, *The Separate Notebooks*

chrysalism

n. the amniotic tranquility of being indoors during a thunderstorm.

Latin *chrysalis*, the pupa of a butterfly. Pronounced "*kris*-uh-liz-uhm."

trumspringa

n. the longing to wander off your career track in pursuit of a simple life—tending a small farm in a forest clearing, keeping a lighthouse on a secluded atoll, or becoming a shepherd in the mountains—which is just the kind of hypnotic diversion that allows your thoughts to make a break for it and wander back to their cubicles in the city.

German *Stadtzentrum*, "city center" + Pennsylvania German *Rumspringa*, "hopping around." Rumspringa is a putative tradition in which Amish teens dip their toes in modernity for a while before choosing whether to commit to the traditional way of life. Pronounced "*truhm*-spring-guh."

kairosclerosis

n. the moment you look around and realize that you're currently happy—consciously trying to savor the feeling—which prompts your intellect to identify it, pick it apart, and put it in context, where it will slowly dissolve until it's little more than an aftertaste.

Ancient Greek καιρός (*kairos*), a sublime or opportune moment + σκλήρωσις (*sklērōsis*), hardening. Pronounced "kahy-roh-skluh-*roh*-sis."

scabulous

adj. proud of a certain scar on your body, which is like an autograph signed to you by a world grateful for your continued willingness to play with her, even if it hurts.

From *scab* + *fabulous*.

occhiolism

n. the awareness of how fundamentally limited your senses are—noticing how little of your field of vision is ever in focus, how few colors you're able to see, how few sounds you're able to hear, and how intrusively your brain fills in the blanks with its own cartoonish extrapolations—which makes you wish you could experience the whole of reality instead of only ever catching a tiny glimpse of it, to just once step back from the keyhole and finally open the door.

Italian *occhiolino* ("little eye"), the original name that Galileo gave to the microscope in 1609. Pronounced "*oh*-kyoh-liz-uhm."

VEMÖDALEN

the fear that originality is no longer possible

You are unique. And you are surrounded by billions of other people, just as unique as you. Each of us is different, with some new angle on the world. So what does it mean if the lives we're busy shaping by hand all end up looking the same?

We all spread out, looking around for scraps of frontier—trying to capture something special, something personal. But when you gather all our scattered snapshots side by side, the results are often uncanny. There's the same close-up of an eye, the same raindrops on a window, the same selfie in the side-view mirror. The airplane wingtip, the pair of bare legs stretched out on a beach chair, the loopy rosette of milk in a latte. The same meals are photographed again and again. The same monuments pinched between fingers. The same waterfalls. Sunset after sunset.

It should be a comfort that we're not so different, that our perspectives so neatly align. If nothing else, it's a reminder that we live in the same world. Still, it makes you wonder. How many of your snapshots could easily be replaced by a thousand identical others? Is there any value left in taking yet another photo of the moon, or the Taj Mahal, or the Eiffel Tower? Is a photograph just a kind of souvenir to prove you've been someplace, like a prefabricated piece of furniture that you happened to have assembled yourself?

It's alright if we tell the same jokes we've all heard before. It's alright if we keep remaking the same movies. It's alright if we keep saying the same phrases to each other as if they had never been said before. Even when you look back to the earliest known work of art in existence, you'll find a handprint stenciled on the wall of a cave—not just one, but hundreds overlapping, each indistinguishable from the other.

To be sure, you and I and billions of others will leave our mark on this world we've inherited, just like the billions who came before us. But if, in the end, we find ourselves with nothing left to say, nothing new to add, idly tracing outlines left by others long ago—it'll be as if we were never here at all.

This too is not an original thought. As the poet once said, "The powerful play goes on, and you will contribute a verse." What else is there to say? When you get your cue, you say your line.

Swedish *vemod*, tender sadness, pensive melancholy + *Vemdalen*, the name of a Swedish town, which is the kind of thing that IKEA usually borrows to give names to their products. Pronounced "*vey*-moh-dah-len."

looseleft

adj. feeling a sense of loss upon finishing a good book, sensing the weight of the back cover locking away the lives of characters you've gotten to know so well.

From *looseleaf*, a removable sheet of paper + *left*, departed.

jouska

n. a hypothetical conversation that you compulsively play out in your head—a crisp analysis, a devastating comeback, a cathartic heart-to-heart—which serves as a kind of psychological batting cage that feels far more satisfying than the small-ball strategies of everyday life.

French *jusqu'à*, until. In baseball, "small ball" is a cautious offensive strategy devoted to getting on base via walks, bunts, and steals, forgoing the big home run moments that fans tend to enjoy. Pronounced "*zhoos*-ka."

plata rasa

n. the lulling sound of a running dishwasher, whose steady maternal shushing somehow puts you completely at peace with not having circumnavigated anything solo.

Latin *plata*, plate + *rasa*, blank or scraped clean. Pronounced "*pla*-tuh *rah*-suh."

slipfast

adj. longing to disappear completely; to melt into a crowd and become invisible, so you can take in the world without having to take part in it—free to wander through conversations without ever leaving footprints, free to dive deep into things without worrying about making a splash.

From *slip*, to move or fly away in secret + *fast*, fortified against attack.

elsewise

adj. struck by the poignant strangeness of other people's homes, which smell and feel so different than your own—seeing the details of their private living space, noticing their little daily rituals, the way they've arranged their things, the framed photos of people you'll never know.

From *else*, other + *wise*, with reference to.

the Til

n. the reservoir of all possible opportunities still available to you at this point in your life—all the countries you still have the energy to explore, the careers you still have the courage to pursue, the skills you still have time to develop, the relationships you still have the heart to make—like a pail of water you carry around in your head, which starts off feeling like an overwhelming burden but steadily draws down as you get older, splashing gallons over the side every time you take a step.

From *the till*, a shopkeeper's register filled with unspent change + *until*.

ASTROPHE

the feeling of being stuck on Earth

It's hard not to look at the ground as you walk. To set your sights low, and keep the world spinning, just trying to stay present wherever you are. But every so often you remember to look up at the stars, and imagine what's out there. Before long, you find yourself grounded once again—grounded in the sense of being housebound, stuck on the planet Earth.

The more you look to the sky, the more you find yourself back on Earth, confronting certain possibilities. It's possible there are other names for our planet that we will never know. That there are constellations that feature our sun, from an angle we'll never get to see. That there are many other civilizations hidden beyond the veil of time, too far away for their light to ever reach us.

We dream of other worlds and name them after old discarded gods, and they seem almost as distant—too far to be seen with the naked eye. Too far even to be seen with our sharpest telescopes, leaning out over the far edge of our atmosphere. They exist only in probabilistic blips in the data, hinting that something must be blocking the starlight at certain intervals. Somehow that's enough to extrapolate entire worlds out there, as if they were ripe for the taking, but many of these distant galaxies and exoplanets will only ever exist in artists' renditions, with the colors tweaked to add a bit of flair.

Even our own solar system is eerily sparse. In textbooks, we tend to print all the planets nested tightly together, because if we tried to draw them to scale, they'd be so small and far apart, they wouldn't even fit in the same room. Even our own moon, which seems to hang so close to Earth, is so far away that all the other planets could fit in the empty space between them. And of all the billions of people on Earth, only twelve of them have ever pushed free and set foot on alien soil.

It's possible that our spacesuits won't need treaded boots ever again. That one day soon we'll tire of exploring and move back home for good. And we'll get used to watching our feet as we walk, occasionally stopping to hurl a single probe into the abyss, like a message in a bottle.

Maybe it shouldn't matter if anyone ever finds it. If nobody's there to know we once lived here on Earth. Maybe it should be like skipping a stone across the surface of a lake. It doesn't matter where it ends up. All that matters is that we're here on the shore—trying to have fun and pass the time, and see how far it goes.

Ancient Greek ἄστρον (*ástron*), star + ἀτροφία (*atrophía*), a wasting away due to lack of use. Pronounced "*as*-truh-fee."

ameneurosis

n. the half-forlorn, half-escapist ache of a train whistle howling in the distance at night.

From *amen*, "so be it" + *neurosis*, an anxious state + *amanuensis*, an assistant who helps transcribe newly composed music. A train whistle is the sound of air being forced across a gap, which serves as a poignant reminder of all the gaps in your life. Pronounced "ah-men-nyoo-*roh*-sis."

volander

n. the ethereal feeling of looking down at the world through an airplane window, able to catch a glimpse of far-flung places you'd never see in person, free to let your mind wander, trying to imagine what they must feel like down on the ground—the closest you'll ever get to an objective point of view.

Latin *volare*, to fly + *solander*, a book-shaped box for storing maps. Pronounced "voh-*land*-uhr."

licotic

adj. anxiously excited to introduce a friend to something you think is amazing—a classic album, a favorite restaurant, a TV show they're lucky enough to watch for the very first time—which prompts you to continually poll their face waiting for the inevitable rush of awe, only to cringe when you discover all the work's flaws shining through for the very first time.

Old English *licode*, it pleased [you] + *psychotic*. Pronounced "lahy-*kot*-ic."

fitzcarraldo

n. a random image that becomes lodged deep in your brain—maybe washed there by a dream, or smuggled inside a book, or planted during a casual conversation—which then grows into a wild and impractical vision that keeps scrambling around in your head, itching for a chance to leap headlong into reality.

From the title character of the 1982 film *Fitzcarraldo*, directed by Werner Herzog, about a man who is overcome by the thought of hearing Caruso's operatic tenor echoing through the Peruvian jungle; to fund this effort he hires local people to pull a steamship over a mountain, a feat that was done for real for the film's production. Pronounced "fits-kuh-*rawl*-doh."

exulansis

n. the tendency to give up trying to talk about an experience because people are unable to relate to it—whether through envy or pity or mere foreignness—which allows it to drift away from the rest of your story, until it feels out of place, almost mythical, wandering restlessly in the fog, no longer even looking for a place to land.

Latin *exulans*, exile, wanderer, derived from the Latin name of the Wandering Albatross, *diomedea exulans*, who spend most of their life in flight, rarely landing, going hours without even flapping their wings. The albatross is a symbol of good luck, a curse, and a burden, and sometimes all three at once. Pronounced "ek-suh-*lan*-sis."

la cuna

n. a twinge of sadness that there's no frontier left, that as the last explorer trudged his armies toward the last blank spot on the map, he didn't suddenly turn for home, leaving one last island unexplored so we could set it aside as a strategic reserve of mystery.

Latin *lacuna*, an unfilled space or hole + Spanish *la cuna*, cradle. Pronounced "lah *koo*-nuh."

Fig. 1. Ozurie. | Collage by Mr. Babies

OZURIE

feeling torn between the life you want
and the life you have

Consider Dorothy, the orphan girl of Kansas, sitting up in her bed at the end of the movie. While the credits roll and the music swells, with the Land of Oz still fading from her eyes, she whispers to herself, "There's no place like home."

Eventually, of course, she knows she'll have to get out of bed, put on a pair of ordinary black slippers, and carry on with her life on the farm. Counting the chicks, darning the stockings, pushing gray eggs around a cast-iron pan. She'll play around with Toto, just as she did before. And when she opens the door, she'll step out into a world of black and white, into a broad sweep of flat land that reaches the edge of the sky in all directions. And she'll know that she's not in Oz anymore. She had her rumspringa and chose to return, which means she is now a confirmed Kansan.

And yet, even as she makes her way to school the next morning, she now carries with her a certain unshakable awareness—that her gray gingham dress is secretly blue, that her charcoal hair is actually a rich auburn, that the sky catches fire when the sun goes down. She'll try to blink the colors out of her eyes, but she'll never be able to forget that there's an entire dimension hidden inside things. Everything will now have a grainy reticence that feels intolerable to her. She knows that this humdrum workaday world can explode without warning, blooming with color and potential and chaos. She alone can sense the shimmer of gold on the gray gravel road, the lion's roar hidden in a friend's voice. She will feel a new dissatisfaction with surfaces and distances, feel the urge to yank open the curtains and rip into people's hearts and set them on fire, just to get a sense of what they're made of.

To her, Oz is more than a dream. It's a sickness. A feverish desire that infected her mind, making normal life feel intolerable, when she had been doing just fine. But where does she go from here? How long will it be before she's gazing over the rainbow once again? How long before she's galloping across the fields like a storm chaser, beckoning her arms to the clouds like a toddler desperate to be picked up?

And even if she gets her wish, and wakes up back in Oz as if no time had passed—what then? How long before she's clicking her heels on the sidewalks of Emerald City, trying to flag down a hot air balloon to take her back to the comfort and safety of home? If Oz is a dream that never leaves you, so is Kansas. Life is not a flat and barren outpost, and it's not a bangarang wonderland either. Maybe they're just two different ways of looking at some ambiguous middle place, where she actually lives. It's just a question of perspective, which can shift wildly depending on how she chooses to see it.

Such is life. Some days you wake up in Kansas, and some days in Oz. Sometimes the world feels pretty much stuck in place, and you've made your peace with that. Why waste time on silly pipe dreams, when there are socks to darn and pigs to feed? At other times, you look around and see how exciting the world can be, how flexible and arbitrary things are, how easy it might be to cast aside your old life and get to work building the one you really want.

Eventually you have to decide what to do with this desire. Do you tamp it down in yourself, or do you chase after it? Should you quit your job to pursue your dream, or hang on to that steady paycheck? Stay in an okay relationship or find a better match? Do you plunge into a Technicolor riot of what might be, harsh and delirious and confusing? Or do you accept the humble beauty of ordinary life, where nothing ever changes, and everything is simple? Which will it be—Kansas or Oz? Life as it is or life as it could be?

Soon enough, life will offer you an answer. But for the moment, you are like Dorothy, sitting up in her bed, trying to decide which pair of slippers she wants to wear today. Black or ruby? Black or ruby? Until she decides, she'll be caught in a maddening state of tension, trying to live in two worlds at once—padding around the farmhouse as it spins inside the twister, with rubies shining in her bloodstream, her auburn hair slowly turning gray.

Spare a thought for poor Dorothy, the orphan girl of Kansas, who dreams in color but lives in black and white.

From *Oz* + *the prairie*, with *you* caught somewhere in between. Pronounced "*oz*-you-ree" or "*ozh*-uh-ree."

idlewild

adj. feeling grateful to be stranded in a place where you can't do much of anything—sitting for hours at an airport gate, the sleeper car of a train, or the backseat of a van on a long road trip—which temporarily alleviates the burden of being able to do anything at any time and frees up your brain to do whatever it wants to do, even if it's just to flicker your eyes across the passing landscape.

From *Idlewild*, the original name of John F. Kennedy International Airport in New York City.

aubadoir

n. the otherworldly atmosphere just before 5 a.m., when the bleary melodrama of an extremely late night becomes awkwardly conflated with the industrious fluorescence of a very early morning.

French *aubade*, an ode to the morning + *abattoir*, slaughterhouse. Pronounced "oh-bah-*dwahr*."

rückkehrunruhe

n. the feeling of returning from an immersive trip only to notice it fading rapidly from your awareness, as if your brain had automatically assumed it was all just a dream and already went to work scrubbing it from your memory.

German *rückkehren*, coming back + *Unruhe*, restlessness. Compare *Zugunruhe*, "migration restlessness," the fidgety behavior observed in birds approaching migration. Pronounced "rook-*kair*-oon-roo-uh."

mahpiohanzia

n. the frustration of being unable to fly, unable to stretch out your arms and vault into the air, having finally shrugged off the burden of your own weight, which you've been carrying your entire life without a second thought.

Lakota *mahpiohanzi*, "a shadow caused by a cloud." Pronounced "mah-pee-oh-*han*-zee-uh."

the kick drop

n. the moment you wake up from an immersive dream and have to abruptly recalibrate to the real world—unquitting your job, falling right back out of love, reburying your lost loved ones.

In American football, the *drop kick* is when a player drops the ball and kicks it as it bounces off the ground, used as a method of restarting play.

MARU MORI

*the heartbreaking simplicity
of ordinary things*

Most living things don't need to remind themselves that life is precious. They simply pass the time. An old cat can sit in the window of a bookstore, whiling away the hours as people wander through. Blinking calmly, breathing in and out, idly watching a van being unloaded across the street, without thinking too much about anything. And that's alright. It's not such a bad way to live.

So much of life is spent this way, in ordinary time. There's no grand struggle, no sacraments, no epiphanies. Just simple domesticity, captured in little images, here and there. All the cheap little objects. The jittering rattle of an oscillating fan; a pair of toothbrushes waiting in a cup by the sink. There's the ragged squeal of an old screen door, the dry electronic screech of a receipt being printed, the ambient roar of someone showering upstairs. And the feeling of pulling on a pair of wool socks on a winter morning and peeling them off at the end of the day. These are sensations that pass without a second thought. So much of it is barely worth noting.

But in a couple hundred years, this world will turn over to a completely different cast of characters. They won't look back and wonder who won the battles or when. Instead, they'll try to imagine how we lived day to day, gathering precious artifacts of the world as it once was, in all its heartbreaking little details. They'll look for the doodles left behind in the margins of our textbooks, and the dandelions pressed in the pages. They'll try to imagine how our clothes felt on our bodies, and what we ate for lunch on a typical day, and what it might've cost. They'll wonder about our superstitions, the weird little memes and phrases and jokes we liked to tell, the pop songs we hummed mindlessly to ourselves. They'll try to imagine how it must've felt to stand on a street corner, looking around at the architecture, hearing old cars rumbling by. The smell in the air. What ketchup must have tasted like.

We rarely think to hold on to that part of life. We don't build statues of ordinary people. We don't leave behind little plaques to commemorate the milestones of ordinary time:

HERE ON THE TWENTY FIFTH OF MARCH

NINETEEN HUNDRED AND NINETY FOUR

SOME NEIGHBORS WENT OUT WALKING THEIR DOGS

THE CHILDREN TOOK TURNS HOLDING THE LEASH

IT WAS A FUN AFTERNOON FOR EVERYONE INVOLVED

But it all still happened. All those cheap and disposable experiences are no less real than anything in our history books, no less sacred than anything in our hymnals. Perhaps we should try keeping our eyes open while we pray, and look for the meaning hidden in the things right in front of us: in the sound of Tic Tacs rattling in a box, the throbbing ache of hiccups, and the punky smell that lingers on your hands after doing the dishes. Each is itself a kind of meditation, a reminder of what is real.

We need these silly little things to fill out our lives, even if they don't mean all that much. If only to remind us that the stakes were never all that high in the first place. It's not always life-and-death. Sometimes it's just life—and that's alright.

A tribute to Maru Mori, a friend of Pablo Neruda, whose gift of wool socks inspired his poem "Ode to My Socks." Compare *memento mori*, a poignant reminder of your own mortality. Pronounced "*mah*-roo *moh*-ree."

vulture shock

n. the nagging sense that no matter how many days you spend exploring a foreign country, you never quite manage to step foot in it—instead floating high above the culture like a diver over a reef, too dazzled by its exotic quirks to notice its problems and complexities and banalities, while drawing from the heavy tank of assumptions that you carry on your back wherever you go.

From *vulture*, an animal that hovers high over its prey + *culture shock*, the confusion of having to adjust to a culture different than the one you're used to.

merrenness

n. the lulling isolation of driving late at night—floating through the void in an otherworldly hum, trailing red jewels in the darkness, your high beams sweeping back and forth like a lighthouse.

Hungarian *merre*, where? in which direction? Pronounced "*mair-uhn-nis*."

justing

n. the habit of telling yourself that just one tweak could solve all of your problems—if only you had the right haircut, if only you found the right group of friends, if only you made a little more money, if only he noticed you, if only she loved you back, if only you could find the time, if only you were confident—which leaves you feeling perpetually on the cusp of a better life, hanging around the top of the slide waiting for one little push.

From *just*, only, simply, merely + *jousting*, a sport won by positioning the tip of your lance at just the right spot, at just the right second. Pronounced "*juhst*-ing."

Fig. 2. Ballagàrraidh. | Collage by Irie Wata

BALLAGÀRRAIDH

the awareness that you are not
at home in the wilderness

Sometimes you move through the city and feel in your bones how strange and new this all is—the spectacle of modern civilization, just barely older than you are, with its cramped logic, its rules and gridlines and rigid justifications for why the world must be the way it is. And there's a part of you that thinks, *You are not at home here.* That still remembers Eden, and longs to return.

The story of humanity is a move from the countryside to the big city. But it's happened so fast that our brains are still stuck in the hinterlands. There's a part of you that longs to leave your car idling in traffic, hop the fence, and flee into the forest. To wander for miles through open territory, forced by fate to live in the moment, your eyes glued to the horizon, your ears tuned to the rustling of leaves. To feel the lushness and harshness of the wild, the clarity of eating and killing and growing stronger. To live off the land without tools or simulations, and experience nature in all its simplicity—raw, indifferent, and ferociously real.

And yet, another part of you knows that Eden is a fantasy. Even our oldest symbols of nature are deeply unnatural: the plants we eat are sterile, swollen, unrecognizable to the food chain. Our domesticated animals are mere caricatures of their wild ancestors. The family dog is just another piece of technology, designed and bred to serve a purpose. And you too are a domesticated animal, shrouded in synthetic fibers and synthetic thoughts. Even if you wander off to sleep in the woods with a stove and a backpack, everything from the buzzing in your ears to the howling in the distance will be trying to tell you, *You are not at home here*. As much as you want to sink your claws into the dirt, you'll always be floating somewhere above it, trailing clouds of civilization wherever you go.

We need to believe in the fall from Eden. We need to believe that we corrupted a place that had always been pure. But maybe all along, we had the story backward. Maybe we were the ones who cast out the jungle, who stripped it naked, and tried to teach it good and evil, breaking it down into pieces that served a purpose. We couldn't handle the true state of nature—the overwhelming chaos, the corruption and the mutations, the fluidity of interconnections and the fecundity of the soil, where nothing is pure, where life and death are intertwined. So we decided to turn away, barricading ourselves in a walled garden.

Maybe we were wrong from the start. In the beginning, there was everything.

Scottish Gaelic *balla gàrraidh*, garden wall. Pronounced "bah-luh-gah-*rahy*" or "bah-lah-*ghaw*-rah."

foreclearing

n. the act of deliberately refusing to learn the scientific explanations of things out of fear that it'll ruin the magic—turning flower petals into tacky billboards, decoding birdsong into trash talk, defracting a rainbow back inside its tiny prism.

Danish *forklaring*, explanation. Pronounced "fohr-*kleer*-ing."

ne'er-be-gone

n. a person who has no idea where their home is, or was, or when they might have left it—which leaves their emotional compass free to swing around wildly as they move from place to place, pulling them everywhere and nowhere all at once, making it that much harder to navigate.

Middle English *naur*, nowhere + *begone*, surrounded. Pronounced "*nair*-bi-gawn."

wildred

adj. feeling the haunting solitude of extremely remote places—a clearing in the forest, a windswept field of snow, a rest area in the middle of nowhere—which makes you feel like you've just intruded on a conversation that had nothing to do with you, where even the gravel beneath your feet and the trees overhead are holding themselves back to a pointed, inhospitable silence.

From *wild* + *dread*. Pronounced "*wil*-drid."

ghough

n. a hollow place in your psyche that can never be filled; a bottomless hunger for more food, more praise, more attention, more affection, more joy, more sex, more money, more hours of sunshine, more years of your life; a state of panic that everything good will be taken from you too early, which makes you want to swallow the world before it ends up swallowing you.

Onomatopoeic to the sound of a devouring maw. Pronounced "hawkh," with air drawn sharply inward through the mouth.

ringlorn

adj. the wish that the modern world felt as epic as the one depicted in old stories and folktales—a place of tragedy and transcendence, of oaths and omens and fates, where everyday life felt like a quest for glory, a mythic bond with an ancient past, or a battle for survival against a clear enemy, rather than an open-ended parlor game where all the rules are made up and the points don't matter.

From *ring*, a key element in many sagas and myths + *-lorn*, sorely missing. Pronounced "*ring*-lawrn."

harmonoia

n. an itchy sense of dread when life feels just a hint too peaceful—when everyone seems to get along suspiciously well, with an eerie stillness that makes you want to brace for the inevitable collapse, or burn it down yourself.

From *harmony* + *paranoia*. Pronounced "hahr-muh-*noi*-uh."

gobo

n. the delirium of having spent all day in an aesthetic frame of mind—watching a beautiful movie, taking photos across the city, getting lost in an art museum—which infuses the world with an aura of meaning, until every crack in the wall becomes a commitment to naturalism, and every rainbow swirling in a puddle feels like a choice.

Short for *go-between*. In theatrical lighting, a *gobo* is a layer inserted into a lamp that shapes the pool of light that hits the stage. Pronounced "*goh*-boh."

treachery of the common

n. the fear that everyone around the world is pretty much the same—that despite our local quirks, we were all mass-produced in the same factory, built outward from the same generic homunculus, preinstalled with the same tribal compulsions and character defects—which would leave you out of options if you ever want to reinvent yourself, or seek out a better society on the other side of the globe.

A riff on *the tragedy of the commons*, which is a situation where individual users acting in their own self-interest end up harming the common good, usually by depletion or pollution of resources.

funkenzwangsvorstellung

n. the primal trance of watching a campfire in the dark.

German *Funken*, spark + *Zwangsvorstellung*, obsession. Pronounced "foon-ken-tsvang-*svohr*-stel-oong."

zielschmerz

n. the dread of finally pursuing a lifelong dream, which requires you to put your true abilities out there to be tested on the open savannah, no longer protected inside the terrarium of hopes and delusions that you started up in kindergarten and kept sealed as long as you could.

German *Ziel*, goal + *Schmerz*, pain. Pronounced "*zeel*-shmerts."

Fig. 3. Onism. | Collage by Adam Lalonde | onlyghosts.com

ONISM

*the awareness of how little of
the world you'll experience*

You can hear it in the Islamic call to prayer at dawn, in the afternoon school bell, in a train whistle howling in the distance at night. It's encoded in the flicker of fluorescent lights, in the lyrics of lullabies, in lottery numbers, and in the word *archipelago*. You can smell it in sunscreen and diesel fumes and old books that fall apart in your hands; taste it in lukewarm champagne and hot blood trickling from a wound on your forehead. It's packed aboard the Voyager spacecraft, currently fleeing our solar system like a flare fired from the deck of a sinking ship. Sometimes you feel it vibrating in your pocket, even when it's not there.

It's a delirious madness built into all living things. Right from the beginning, each of us has to confront a certain fundamental paradox: in order to be anywhere, you have to be somewhere. You have to confine yourself to just one body, inhabiting only one place at a time. This is the only perspective you'll ever have, the only stretch of history you'll ever get to see for yourself. Even though you may be lucky enough to serve as a witness to the universe, you're cursed by the knowledge that you can only scratch the surface of it. You feel like those first explorers, thousands of years ago, who drew their maps right to the edge of the known world and had to make their peace with vast stretches of blank space.

It's strange how little of the world you actually get to see. No matter where on Earth you happen to be standing, the horizon you see in the distance is only ever about three miles away from you, a bit less than five kilometers. Which means that at any given time, you're barely more than an hour's walk from a completely different world. Alas, even if you lace up your boots and take off for the hills, the circle of your horizon will follow you around like a prison searchlight. The gravel under your feet will always look gritty and literal; the mountains in the distance will always seem bluish and otherworldly. Which means your surroundings will always be infused with a certain ambivalence. Maybe this is where you belong—or maybe there's something far better just over the next ridge. Without calibrating your perspective to the breadth of all possible options, you have no way of knowing. You'll always have to wonder.

Still, most of the time you manage to keep your focus on the bright circle of your immediate experience, while your brain gets to work building a mental picture of everything you might be missing, doodling away in the blank spaces on the map. It starts by extrapolating outward from the world you know—if you've seen one little town, you've seen them all—and fills out the remainder with a collage of secondhand accounts and postcard snapshots. You may never make it to Egypt, but you've already built the pyramids inside your head. You might've only seen a few samurai movies and anime shows, but still assume you have a half-decent understanding of Japanese culture. In this way you build yourself a mental model of what lies beyond your horizon. It's not perfect, but it's good enough to fill in the blanks. Sometimes all you need is a single word on a map—*Tuanaki*, *Saxenburgh*, *Antillia*—and your mind fills up with visions of what might be out there.

But sometimes late at night you look out at the lights flickering in the distance, just on the edge of the horizon, and find yourself struggling to imagine the alternate universe that each of them represents. You think of all the places you'll never have time to explore, some of which might feel like the home you never had, or like a living hell, or like walking around on another planet. You might one day be able to visit one or two or ten of these places, but you'll never be able to shake the feeling that with every step you take, a thousand more lights will appear, and a thousand more, and a thousand more. It's as if you're standing in front of the departures screen in an airport, flickering over with so many exotic place names, each representing one more path you could explore or one more thing you'll never get to see before you die—and all because, as the arrow on the map helpfully points out, *you are here.*

It's strange to think that some of those lights in the distance might be looking right back at you, just barely able to make out the lamp shining over your back door from three miles away. There might even be a few people peering down from a plane passing overhead, wondering to themselves what it's like to be standing right where you're standing, and they might even be feeling a sense of loss, knowing they'll never have time to explore your corner of the world. But then they'll banish the thought; they can already picture it clearly in their heads.

We all know that there's no such thing as a tropical paradise, or hell on Earth. That faraway people are neither angelic monks nor snarling grotesques, that their lives are just as messy and troubled and mundane as our own. But like the first explorers, we can't help ourselves from sketching monsters in the blank spaces on the map. Perhaps we find their presence comforting. They guard the edges of the abyss, and force us to look away, so we can live comfortably in the known world, at least for a little while.

But if someone were to ask you on your deathbed what it was like to live here on Earth, perhaps the only honest answer would be: "I don't know. I passed through it once, but I've never really been there."

In philosophy, *monism* is the belief that a wide variety of things can be explained in terms of a single reality, substance, or source. *Onism* is a kind of monism—your life is indeed limited to a single reality by virtue of being restricted to a single body—but something is clearly missing. Pronounced "*oh*-niz-uhm."

TWO

The Interior Wilderness

DEFINING WHO YOU ARE
FROM THE INSIDE OUT

This is what I believe:

"That I am I."

"That my soul is a dark forest."

"That my known self will never be more than a little clearing in the forest."

"That gods, strange gods, come forth from the forest into the clearing of my known self, and then go back."

"That I must have the courage to let them come and go."

"That I will never let mankind put anything over me, but that I will try always to recognize and submit to the gods in me and the gods in other men and women."

There is my creed.

—D. H. LAWRENCE,
Studies in Classic American Literature

heartspur

n. an unexpected surge of emotion in response to a seemingly innocuous trigger—the distinctive squeal of a rusty fence, a key change in an old pop song, the hint of a certain perfume—which feels all the more intense because you can't quite pin it down.

From *heart* + *spur*, a spike on a heel that urges a horse to move forward.

vaucasy

n. the fear that you're little more than a product of your circumstances, that for all the thought you put into shaping your beliefs and behaviors and relationships, you're essentially a dog being trained by whatever stimuli you happen to encounter—reflexively drawn to whoever gives you reliable hits of pleasure, skeptical of ideas that make you feel powerless.

From Jacques de Vaucanson, a French engineer who built a series of lifelike programmable machines (automata), including his masterpiece the *Digesting Duck*, which could flap its wings and quack, drink water, and digest bits of grain into simulated excrement. Pronounced "*vaw-kuh-see*."

liberosis

n. the desire to care less about things; to figure out a way to relax your grip on your life and hold it loosely and playfully, keeping it in the air like a volleyball, with quick and fleeting interventions, bouncing freely in the hands of trusted friends, always in play.

Italian *libero*, free. A *libero* is a position on a volleyball team that can move at greater liberty than other players, subbing freely and without permission, with an emphasis on keeping the ball in play. Pronounced "lib-er-*oh*-sis."

emodox

n. someone whose mood is perpetually out of sync with everyone else around them, prone to feelings of naptime panic, heart-to-heart snark, or dance club pensiveness.

From *emotional* + *dox*, not conforming to expected norms. Pronounced "*ee*-moh-doks."

nighthawk

n. a recurring thought that only seems to strike you late at night—an overdue task, a nagging guilt, a looming future—which you sometimes manage to forget for weeks, only to feel it land on your shoulder once again, quietly building a nest.

Nighthawks is a famous painting by Edward Hopper, depicting a lonely corner diner late at night. In logging, a *nighthawk* is a metal ball that slid up and down a riverboat's flagpole, to aid pilots in navigation.

the giltwrights

n. the imaginary committee of elders that keeps a running log of all your mistakes, steadily building their case that you're secretly a fraud, a coward, a doofus, and a douche— who would've revoked your good fortune years ago had they not been hampered by their own bitter squabblings over proper grammar and spelling.

Old English *gilt*, awareness of wrongdoing + *wrought*, shaped with hammers. Pronounced "the *gilt*-rahyts."

nementia

n. the post-distraction effort to recall the reason you're feeling particularly anxious or angry or excited, trying to retrace your sequence of thoughts like a kid gathering the string of a downed kite.

Ancient Greek νέμειν (*némein*), to give what is due + Latin *dementia*, without mind. Pronounced "ne-*men*-shuh."

the whipgraft delusion

n. the phenomenon in which you catch your reflection in the mirror and get the sense that you're peering into the eyes of a stranger, as if you're looking at a police sketch of your own face aged forward twenty years, which would imply that the real you is out there somewhere, wandering the streets of your old neighborhood, still at large.

In horticulture, *whip grafting* is when you fuse the top of one plant to the bottom of another. In psychology, *the Capgras delusion* is the conviction that a loved one has been replaced by an identical-looking imposter.

deep gut

n. a resurgent emotion that you hadn't felt in years, that you might have forgotten about completely if your emotional playlist hadn't accidentally been left on shuffle.

In music, a *deep cut* is a lesser-known track that only an artist's true fans or completists might appreciate.

KOINOPHOBIA

the fear that you've lived an ordinary life

While you're in it, life seems epic. Fiery, tenuous, and unpredictable. But when you look back over your story, or try to put it down on paper, you can see more of it at once than ever before—and yet it seems somehow diminished. Humble. Almost quaint.

So you begin scanning your life, looking for something interesting or beautiful. You see an ordinary house, on an ordinary street. It looks smaller than you remember. You once had wild dreams and obstacles and risks looming all around you, but now those look smaller, too. You remember giants and goddesses and villains, but now all you see are ordinary people, assembled in their tiny classrooms and workspaces, each moving around in little steps, like tokens on a game board.

No matter how many times you rolled the dice, it was always these little moves, here and there. Do a little work. Take a little rest. Make a little friend. Throw a little party. Feel a little boredom. Have a little rebellion. There are so many of these token moments, that you could have sworn were supposed to represent something else, something bigger. You keep adding them all up, as if there were something you must've forgotten to count, some stash of glory that fell off the back of a truck.

You may well adore the life you have for everything it is. You know it isn't groundbreaking, but you wouldn't change a thing. Still, you can't shake the feeling that something is missing.

Maybe the trouble is, you were never really "in it" to begin with. Maybe when you first started building the life you wanted, you put so much thought into what might happen that you started losing sight of what was happening. As if you had known all along that this wasn't the world you expected. A world so low and common that you tried to keep your distance, so you began floating somewhere above it, where nobody else could look down on this life you built. That is, nobody else but you.

Ancient Greek κοινός (*koinós*), common, ordinary, stripped of specialness + -φοβία (*-phobía*), fear. Pronounced "key-noh-*foh*-bee-uh."

keep

n. an important part of your personality that others seldom see—a secret flaw, a hidden talent, trauma that never comes up, dreams you never mention—that remains a vital part of who you are even if nobody knows it's there, like the sprawling archives in the attics of museums, packed with works far too priceless to risk being displayed for the public.

From a *keep*, the innermost tower of a castle.

agnosthesia

n. the state of not knowing how you really feel about something, which forces you to sift through clues hidden in your own behavior, as if you were some other person—noticing a twist of acid in your voice, an obscene amount of effort you put into something trifling, or an inexplicable weight on your shoulders that makes it difficult to get out of bed.

Ancient Greek ἄγνωστος (*ágnōstos*), not knowing + διάθεσις (*diáthesis*), condition, mood. Pronounced "ag-nos-*thee*-zhuh."

trueholding

n. the act of trying to keep an amazing discovery to yourself, fighting the urge to shout about it from the rooftops because you're afraid that it'll end up being diluted and distorted, and will no longer have been created just for you.

In the Tolkien legendarium, *Trahald* is the true name of Sméagol (Gollum), a creature who spent centuries hiding in dark wet caves, enthralled in jealous worship of his precious enchanted ring.

punt kick

n. a quiet jolt of recognition that it's time to become a better version of yourself, sensing that all the strategies that brought you this far are no longer working—that it's not enough anymore to be cute or nice or righteous or tough—as if you've now entered a new phase in the game of life, moving forward with a completely different token.

Dutch *puntstuk*, railway frog, which is the part of a railway switch where two rails intersect. Sometimes you can feel a little kick when your train passes over it, as if the world is trying to signal you're missing a turn, having traveled too far on the same old track.

fool's guilt

n. a pulse of shame you feel even though you've done nothing wrong—passing a police car while under the speed limit, being carded after legally ordering a drink, or exiting a store without buying anything.

From *fool's gold* + *guilt*. Also known as a *reverse Alford plea,* whereby you plead innocent to all charges but want the judge to know that you feel kinda guilty anyway.

endzoned

n. the hollow feeling of having gotten exactly what you thought you wanted, only to learn that it didn't make you happy.

In sports, the *endzone* is the final goal, the end of the line—but at a certain point you have to drop the ball.

candling

v. intr. the habit of taking stock of your life on the occasion of your birthday—letting it serve as a kind of internal referendum on all your goals and qualities and relationships and accomplishments so far—which makes you want to dress just a little nicer that day, as if you're standing before a parole board that convenes once a year to adjudicate your release from childhood.

From *candling*, a method of egg inspection in which an egg is backlit with a candle flame to reveal how the chick is growing, or if it's there at all.

altschmerz

n. a sense of weariness with the same old problems that you've always had, the same boring issues and anxieties you've been gnawing on for decades, which makes you want to spit them out and dig up some fresher pain you might have buried in your mental backyard.

German *alt*, old + *Schmerz*, pain. Pronounced "*alt*-shmerts."

lyssamania

n. the irrational fear that someone you know is angry at you, that as soon as you wander into the room, you'll be faced with a barrage of questions that gradually escalates into a frenzy of outrage, for reasons that you don't understand.

In Ancient Greek mythology, the *Maniae* are spirits who personified insanity, along with their sister *Lyssa,* who was known for erupting into rages. Pronounced "lis-uh-*mey*-nee-uh."

tarrion

n. an odd interval of blankness you feel after something big happens to you but before you feel the resulting emotional reaction—stunned by a sudden loss, a stroke of luck, or an unexpected visitor—like those tension-filled seconds between a flash of lightning and the thunderclap that follows, which gives you a hint of how near you are to the coming storm.

From *tarry,* to be late to react, or linger in expectation + *carry on.* Pronounced "*tar*-ee-uhn."

wellium

n. an excuse you come up with to rationalize a disappointing outcome—telling yourself you weren't in the mood for that sold-out show anyway, that your safety school is actually a better fit, that your dream job might have been a bit too stressful.

From the phrase "Well, I . . . um . . . ," which typically precedes such an excuse. Pronounced "*wel*-ee-uhm."

KUDOCLASM

a cascading crisis of self-doubt

A warning to Icarus, as he stretched out his wings for the first time: "Don't fly too near the sun, nor the sea. One will melt the wax, and the other weigh down the feathers. Keep to the middle course."

Most of the time your confidence carries on something like that, in a kind of self-correcting balance. Some days you wake up with your head in the clouds and you have to remind yourself to stay grounded. Other days you're just barely slogging through, hoping something can lift your spirits. But it's not always that simple. Sometimes you have no idea what to think about yourself, feeling somehow better than everybody but not good enough for anybody. Which is actually when you're at your most precarious, feeling overdue for a correction. Something throws you off-balance, and you slip into a spiraling self-doubt—picking apart your wings, trying to figure out if your feathers are still attached.

You think over your life and realize how much of it is mythology, stories you tell yourself. How many half-hearted compliments have you taken to heart, how many of your friendships are kept together by little more than circumstance? You may love your partner but start to doubt how well that comes across. You may love your job but begin to question if it's worth all the time it has cost you, knowing how easily your role could be refilled, your legacy tossed in a box. You wonder if you're really any good at it, or have been ignoring warning signs that it's time to try something else.

But what else could you try? How much do you really know about your interests? Do you actually like the things you like? What makes you happy? Surely it should be enough to sit by a pond in the park, watching the ducks, living in the moment. But what does that do for anybody? Where is the line between self-actualization and self-indulgence? How much of your time could be better spent trying to make a difference? Then again, what difference could you realistically hope to make? Perhaps you tell yourself it doesn't matter as long as you do something—but wouldn't that only prove you were doing it just for yourself, not for some greater cause? So where does that leave you?

You begin to wonder if you've spent your entire life buoyed by airy delusions, coasting along on unearned confidence. But if it's possible to carry on that way indefinitely and not even notice, does it even matter whether any of it is real?

Maybe your self-mythology is no different than any other mythology. It's a story that changes in the telling, evolving over time. Whatever resonates will stay, and what doesn't will fall away. To pick away at the literal truth is to miss the point of it, miss the joy of it. So go ahead and build your myth. Try to tell a good story about yourself that captures something *true*, whether or not the facts agree.

Keep to the middle course. Steal bits of wax and feathers discarded by other, better fliers. Let the sun rise and fall. Let the waves pound themselves to mist, again and again. Your task is not to be flawless. Your task is to fly.

Ancient Greek κῦδος (*kûdos*), glory, praise + κλάω, (*kláō*), to break down. Pronounced "*koo*-doh-klaz-uhm."

maugry

adj. afraid that you've been mentally deranged all your life and everybody around you knows, but none of them mention it to you directly because they feel it's not their place.

From *maunder*, to mumble indistinctly + *maugre*, in spite of, notwithstanding. Pronounced "*maw*-gree."

typifice

n. a caricature of yourself that went out of date years ago, though nobody around you seems to have noticed.

Italian *tipi fissi*, "fixed types," the stock characters in commedia dell'arte masked improvisational theater. Pronounced "*tip*-uh-fis."

proluctance

n. the paradoxical urge to avoid doing something you've been looking forward to—opening a decisive letter, meeting up with a friend who's finally back in town, reading a new book from your favorite author—perpetually waiting around for the right state of mind, stretching out the bliss of anticipation as long as you can.

Latin *pro-*, forward + *reluctans*, resisting. Pronounced "proh-*luhk*-tuhns."

viadne

n. alienation from the crude machinery of your own body—like riding a ramshackle parade float that's run by gremlins you can't see, who toil away in darkness, pulling strings to move your limbs, kneading your guts and working the bellows, trying to further your modern agenda using nothing more advanced than a sackful of bones and splanchnic ganglia, zapped by sparks in primordial ooze.

Latin *via*, by way of + *viande*, meat. Pronounced "vee-*ad*-nee."

aesthosis

n. the state of feeling trapped inside your own subjective tastes—not knowing *why* you find certain things beautiful or ugly, only that you do—wishing you could remove the sociopsychological lenses from your eyes so you could see the beauty in anything and be moved to tears by the smell of burning garbage, the aria of a screaming toddler, or a neon Elvis painted on black velvet.

From *aesthetic*, concerned with beauty or artistry + *orthosis*, a brace that artificially straightens a weak or injured part of the body. Pronounced "es-*thoh*-sis."

loss of backing

n. an abrupt collapse of trust in yourself—having abandoned a resolution, surrendered to your demons, or squandered an opportunity you swore you'd take seriously this time—which resets your expectations and makes it that much harder to guarantee that your word is worth anything, even to yourself.

In economics, a *loss of backing* is when the government no longer guarantees the value of a certain currency, particularly when it's not exchangeable for anything physical like gold or silver, thus it only retains value because we say it does.

malotype

n. a certain person who embodies all the things you like the least about yourself—a seeming caricature of your worst tendencies—which leaves you feeling repulsed and fascinated in equal measure, having stumbled upon a role model of exactly the kind of person you never want to be.

Latin *malus*, bad + *typus*, a kind of sculptor's mold. A mold is essentially a negative image of the object you want to sculpt—so if you're trying to shape yourself, perhaps a good first step is to scoop away the negative space. Pronounced "*mal*-uh-tahyp."

rubatosis

n. the unsettling awareness of your own heartbeat, whose tenuous muscular throbbing feels less like a metronome than a nervous ditty your heart is tapping to itself, as if to casually remind the outside world, *I'm here, I'm here, I'm here.*

In music, *tempo rubato,* "stolen time," is a slight speeding up and slowing down of the tempo of a piece, borrowing time from one measure then paying it back later. Pronounced "roo-bah-*toh*-sis."

leidenfreude

n. a sense of paradoxical relief when something bad happens to you, which temporarily lowers your own expectations for yourself, transforming a faceless protagonist into something of an underdog, who's that much easier to root for.

German *Leiden,* suffering + *Freude,* joy. Compare *Schadenfreude,* joy at the misfortune of others. Pronounced "*lahyd*-n-froi-duh."

elsing

n. the unconscious habit of looking at someone and seeing only a cartoon of what they represent to you, their face obscured by a superimposed image of someone else entirely—your mother, your school bully, or yourself in another time—which makes you wonder what others must see when they look at you from across the room.

From *else.* Pronounced "*el*-sing."

1202

n. the tipping point when your brain becomes so overwhelmed with tasks you need to do, you feel too guilty to put anything off until later, prioritizing every little thing at the top of the list, leaving you immobilized.

During the lunar descent of Apollo 11, the "1202" alarm sounded just before landing, indicating that the computer was receiving more data than it could process. Pronounced "twelve oh two."

the meantime

n. the moment of realization that your quintessential future self isn't ever going to show up, which forces the role to fall upon the understudy, the gawky kid who spent years mouthing their lines in the wings before being shoved into the glare of your life, which is already well into its second act.

From *mean*, common, humble, low-grade + *the meantime*, the time spent waiting for some other event to occur.

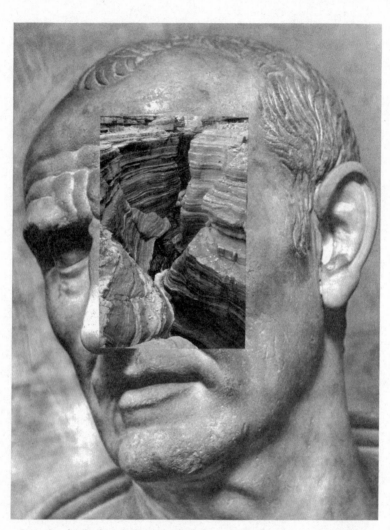

Fig. 4. Alazia. | Collage by Andrés Gamiochipi | andresgamiochipi.com | Instagram @andresgamiochipi

ALAZIA

*the fear that you're no longer
able to change*

When you were born, you could have been anybody. So quick and malleable, your parents could look at your face and see a future president. They tried to mold you as you grew, but they could only work with what they had. And when their tools stopped working, they gradually handed them off to you, asking, "What do you want to be when you grow up?"

There's a certain art to becoming who you are. There's no standard kit you can use to assemble yourself, swapping out parts as needed. Instead, it feels more like a kind of stretching, a teasing out at the edges, like a glassblower standing at the furnace.

A teenage personality is a delicate medium, its emotions almost too heavy to handle. You had to figure out a way to keep yourself together and tease out the good parts without falling out of balance or stretching yourself too thin. You couldn't stop everything to try to fix your flaws, but you couldn't just ignore them either. Luckily, you were nothing if not flexible, softened by the heat of youth, which kept you warm on a dingy couch or a night in the wilderness. You knew that you weren't just you, you were also the person you would one day become. So even when you failed, you could still be whatever you wanted to be. As long as you kept moving.

Inevitably you got hit, and you got hurt. You prided yourself on how well you absorbed the blow, bouncing back as if nothing had happened. But the pain changed you, in little chips and cracks that might take you years to notice. Over time you learned how to position yourself in very specific ways, protecting the most vulnerable parts of your psyche, even as you knew they were still a crucial part of the real you. Gradually you became more and more reluctant to move from that position. Growing a little harder, a little more brittle.

And now here you are. Sometimes you find yourself wondering if you can change, even if you wanted to. If you still have enough fire in the belly to surprise yourself, or if you're already set in your ways, too tough and cynical to stretch without shattering. Maybe you spent so long wondering who you were going to be one day, you forgot that that question actually has an answer, and that "one day" would soon arrive.

Maybe it's too late for you to change who you are. Or maybe you're just entering a new phase, undergoing a change so profound that even your understanding of *change* is becoming unrecognizable. Maybe now is the time to stress-test your own assumptions about yourself, stripping away all the flourishes and ornaments that you don't really need, honing yourself down to the core of who you are. And even if it's true that you're no longer flexible enough to be anybody, you might be getting strong enough to finally be yourself.

Greek αλλάζω (*allázo*), to change + *dysplasia*, abnormal development of tissue. Pronounced "uh-*ley*-zhuh" or "ah-*ley*-zee-uh."

the wends

n. the frustration that you're not enjoying an experience as much as you should, which prompts you to try plugging in various thought combinations to trigger anything more intense than roaring static, as if your heart had been inadvertently demagnetized by a surge of expectations.

From *wend*, to wander unpredictably along a predetermined path. Compare *the bends*, which occurs when a diver ascends too quickly and gas bubbles begin to form in their tissues, a condition that can be debilitating or fatal.

apolytus

n. the moment you realize you are changing as a person, finally outgrowing your old problems like a reptile shedding its skin, already able to twist back around and chuckle at this weirdly antiquated caricature of yourself that will soon come off completely.

From *apolysis*, the stage of molting when an invertebrate's shell begins to separate from the skin beneath it + *adultus*, sacrificed. Pronounced "ah-*pahl*-i-tuhs."

the standard blues

n. the dispiriting awareness that the twists and turns of your life feel new and profound but are not unique—marked by the same coming-of-age struggles as millions of others, the same career setbacks, the same family strife, the same learning curve of parenting—which makes even your toughest challenges feel harmless and predictable, just another remake of the same old story.

A riff on *blues standards*, the catalog of the most popular songs in the blues genre, which is itself famous for chord progressions that cycle through variations on a theme.

mcfeely

adj. inexplicably moved by predictable and well-worn sentiments, even if they're trite or obvious or being broadcast blindly to the masses.

From the middle name of Mr. Fred McFeely Rogers. You deserve to be happy. Your feelings matter. You are loved. You are enough.

ioia

n. the wish that you could see statistics overlaid on every person you encounter—checking the signal strength of their compatibility, a measure of their trustworthiness, or even just an emoji that tells you how they're really feeling.

From the two symbols of binary code, *1* and *0*, denoting "on" or "off" + *I am.* Pronounced "ahy-*yo*-yuh."

flichtish

adj. nervously aware how much of your self-image is based on untested assumptions about yourself—only ever guessing how you'd react to a violent threat, a sudden windfall, a huge responsibility, or being told to do something you knew was wrong.

North Frisian *flicht*, maybe. Pronounced "*flik*-tish."

insoucism

n. the inability to decide how much sympathy your situation really deserves, knowing that so many people have it far worse and others far better, that some people would need years of therapy to overcome what you have, while others would barely think to mention it in their diary that day.

French *soucis*, worries + *insouciance*, indifference. Who knows what an ordinary person should be expected to handle? Perhaps human life is so tough that we all deserve some sympathy. Or perhaps it's such a privilege to be alive at all that none of us has the right to complain. Pronounced "in-*soo*-siz-uhm."

ANOSCETIA

the anxiety of not knowing "the real you"

Everyone around you seems to have such a vibrant color of personality. It shines through vividly in everything they do, from the shoes they wear, to the groceries they put in their cart, to the precise wording of a text wishing you a happy birthday. You'd think it would all seem generic, but somehow every detail is quintessentially *them*.

How strange, then, that your own experience doesn't seem to be tinted with any particular vibe. Mostly you feel you do what you have to do, with little opportunity for embellishment. And when there is free rein to improvise, you find yourself feeding off other people's moods, matching their tones and energies, just trying to get along or make it through the day. Inside your head, you imagine yourself as a shade of neutral gray that just happens to reflect whatever strong colors are nearby.

Of course, your family and friends would insist you're anything but neutral, painting you with the same broad brush you use to paint them: you're a sunny yellow, they might say, or a chill blue, a fiery red, an innocent pink, an edgy black. They're not necessarily wrong; you do notice a certain quality threaded through your personality, and often find yourself playing into it, because it's a lot easier to be cheerful or crabby or crazy or boring if everyone already thinks of you that way. The trouble is, each of them only ever sees you in isolated contexts, inhabiting certain roles at certain times. If anyone tried to shadow you through an entire week, they'd be astonished to see you as a serious professional, a sexual being, a spiritual person, a story-time goofball, a nervous wreck, or the life of the party. Each of their impressions may be accurate in the moment, but each reflects only a narrow band of the full spectrum of you.

Meanwhile, you shadow yourself twenty-four hours a day, in a variety of different situations. In what context are you most like yourself? Are you more or less authentic when you lose yourself in your work, pour your heart out to a friend, or are alone, just trying to clear your mind? Even then, you know firsthand how messy your moods can be, how scattered and contradictory your thought process, how many arbitrary urges you could obey at any given time. Whenever you stumble on a new situation, it's hard to predict which version of you is going to emerge, or which opinion is going to tumble out from the gumball machine in your head—knowing it'll carry the sheen of truth, as if all your other thoughts didn't exist.

It makes you wish you could restore your self-image back to its essence. Painstakingly washing away the remnants of all the times you tried to be someone you're not. Cleaning up areas where people tried to paint over you or ripped away qualities they didn't like. Stripping down your identity, layer by layer, through all your habits and distractions and cultural programming, so you can finally reveal your true colors for all to see. But the more you look into who you are in isolation, the more your identity dissolves into a noise of random impulses—dust on a blank canvas.

Maybe there is no single self to speak of. Maybe you're a shifting collage of many different personas, each as authentic as the next. A kaleidoscope of ever-moving fragments, reflecting a thousand little impressions of the world around you, with flashes of different moods and vibrant clusters of quirks—but no broader pattern.

Maybe you have no true colors. You're not some finished painting, signed and sealed in varnish. If there is a "real you," surely it's the mess of paint on the palette: colors swirling and mixing and playing together, perpetually unfinished, searching and striving to make something new.

From *an-*, not + Latin *Nosce te ipsum*, "Know thyself." Pronounced "an-oh-*see*-sha" or "an-oh-*say*-tyah."

desanté

n. the brooding delirium of being sick, which makes time slow to a trickle and turns even the most pathetic of tasks into monumental struggles, until the act of lifting your head from the pillow feels like trying to climb a mountain, wondering if you'll ever find your way back again, or even catch your breath.

A riff on the French toast *santé*. Literally, "un-health!" Pronounced "day-sahn-*tey*."

sayfish

n. a sincere emotion that seems to wither into mush as soon as you try to put it into words—like reeling in a shimmering beast from the deep only to watch it wriggle limply on the line, which makes you want to leave it down there, languishing unexpressed, where it'll grow dark and slender and weird, with ghostly blue eyes and long translucent teeth.

The *sailfish* is a species of fish noted for its violent power, its eponymous signaling fin, and its ability to change colors like a chameleon. It's also known as the *boohoo*.

addleworth

adj. unable to settle the question of whether you're doing okay in life; feeling torn between conflicting value systems and moveable goalposts, which makes you long for someone to come along and score your progress in discrete and measurable units—points, dollars, friends, followers, or a grade point average—which may not clear up where you're going but would at least reassure you that you're one step closer to getting there.

From *addled,* muddled or unclear + *worth*.

symptomania

n. the fantasy that there's some elaborate diagnosis out there that neatly captures the kind of person you are, tying together your many flaws and contradictions into a single theme—which wouldn't necessarily sort out the mess inside your head but would at least let you mark it with a little sign so people know to walk around it.

From *symptom* + *mania*.

fitching

v. intr. compulsively turning away from works of art you find frustratingly, nauseatingly good—wanting to shut off the film and leave the theater, or devour a book only in maddening little chunks—because it resonates at precisely the right frequency to rattle you to your core, which makes it mildly uncomfortable to be yourself.

From *bitching*, markedly good + *fitch*, the European polecat, an animal that often cripples its prey by piercing its brain with its teeth, before storing it alive in its burrow to return and eat sometime later.

solysium

n. the unhinged delirium of being alone for an extended period of time—feeling the hours stretch into days until a weird little culture begins to form inside your head, with its own superstitions and alternate histories and a half-mumbled dialect all your own—whose freewheeling absurdity feels oddly liberating but makes it that much harder to reacclimate to the strictures and ambiguities of normal social life.

From *solitary*, being by oneself + *asylum*, a sanctuary for the mentally ill + *Elysium*, the Ancient Greek equivalent of heaven. Pronounced "soh-*lee*-zee-uhm."

indosentia

n. the fear that your emotions might feel profound but are crudely biological, less to do with meaning and philosophy than with hormones, endorphins, sleep cycles, and blood sugar—any of which might easily be tweaked to induce unfalsifiable feelings of joy, depression, bloodlust, or kinship, or even a spiritual transcendence of your physical body.

Acronym of the supposed "happy chemicals" Dopamine, Oxytocin, Serotonin, and Endorphins + *in absentia*, something done in your absence. Pronounced "in-duh-*sen*-shah" or "in-doh-*sen*-tyah."

vicarous

adj. curious to know what someone else would do if they were in your shoes, eager to watch another actor put their own spin on the character of You—carrying your body differently, speaking in a tone you never use, saying and doing things you didn't even know were an option—a performance that might well end in disaster but would at least remind you that there are many different ways to play this role, even though you tend to assume you're just reading the lines as written.

From *vicarious*, but without the *I*. Pronounced "*vik*-er-uhs."

bareleveling

v. intr. trying to improve yourself without anyone else knowing about it, afraid that they'll think it's silly or grandiose or unnecessary, or that they'll end up calling too much attention to your efforts, transforming a casual tweak into a flashy rebranding campaign.

Armenian բարելավվել (*barelavvel*), to become better. Pronounced "*bair*-lev-uhl-ing."

hiddled

adj. feeling the loneliness of having to keep a secret to yourself.

Old English *hidil*, hiding place. Pronounced "*hid*-ld."

manusia

n. the ambient feeling of being a human being; a baseline mood that everyone feels intensely every moment of their lives, but can never pin down because they have nothing else to compare it to.

Sanskrit *manusyá*, human being. Pronounced "muh-*noo*-zhuh" or "muh-*noo*-zee-uh."

povism

n. the frustration of being stuck inside your own head, unable to see your face or read your body language in context, only ever guessing how you might be coming across—which makes you think of yourself as a detached observer squinting out at a lushly painted landscape, though to everyone else you seem woven right into the canvas.

From *point of view* + *ism*. Blessed are the slugs, whose eyes are held aloft on wriggling stalks, just tall enough to see their entire bodies in context. Pronounced "*poh*-viz-uhm."

Fig. 5. Ambedo. | Collage by Paul Abrams | *Coffee with a Splash of Milky Way*

AMBEDO

a momentary trance of emotional clarity

Sometimes when you're alone and everything is quiet, you feel a certain placeless intensity that drifts in like a fog. It's subtle at first, lingering somewhere between fidgety boredom and accidental meditation. Maybe you're sitting up in bed on a dark morning before the day begins, staring blankly at a spot on the wall, thinking about life. Or you've arrived somewhere a few minutes early to pick someone up, and you turn off the car and find yourself alone with your thoughts. You take a breath and look around at the still life of the parking lot: a few shrubs swaying in the wind, the arrhythmic tinking of the cooling engine, the keys still swinging in the ignition.

You begin to sense that something is happening—as when you notice a movie pushing into a close-up but can't figure out what it is you're supposed to be taking from it. Details that usually strike you as banal now seem utterly alien. The stitching on your shoes, the tendons moving inside your wrists. The saplings, reaching. How delicate and fleeting it all seems, everything struggling just to exist. You feel a kind of melancholic trance sweeping over you. A rush of clarity, as if you've shaken yourself out of a dream. You are here. You are alive. You are *in it*.

You look around at all the other people who happen to share this corner of the world, and imagine where they came from, marveling that all of their paths managed to cross at this particular point in time. You think back to the series of events that brought you here, your choices and your mistakes and your achievements, such as they are. All the twists and turns over the years. It wasn't what you thought it would be, and yet you can still look back on all the things you've lost, and the opportunities that came and went, and feel a pang of gratitude that it happened at all. And now here you are, feeling a kind of joyful grief for your life, in all its blessings and mysteries and chances and changes.

You look around with a new sense of gratitude, taking in the complexity of things: raindrops skittering down a window, tall trees leaning in the wind, clouds of cream swirling in your coffee. Everything falls quiet, and the words start to lose their meaning. It all seems to mix together, until you can't tell the difference between the ordinary and the epic. And you remember that you too are a guest on this Earth. Your life is not just a quest, or an opportunity, or a story to tell; it's also just an experience, to be lived for its own sake. It doesn't have to mean anything other than what it is. A single moment can still stand on its own, as a morsel of existence.

But after a minute or two, you'll feel your hand reaching for your phone or the car radio, eager to drown out your thoughts with distractions. Perhaps there's a part of you that's instinctively wary of lingering too long in any one moment.

We can breathe this world in, and hold on to it as long as we can, but we can't just stop there. We have to keep moving, digging around for some deeper meaning, hoping to find an escape hatch between one experience and the next. So we never feel stuck inside one little moment, one little life.

Latin *ambedo*, "I sink my teeth into." Pronounced "am-*bee*-doh."

THREE

Montage of Attractions

FINDING SHELTER IN
THE PRESENCE OF OTHERS

Collage by Federica Colletti | Instagram @nonsuperareledosiconsigliate

Life will break you. Nobody can protect you from that, and living alone won't either, for solitude will also break you with its yearning. You have to love. You have to feel. It is the reason you are here on earth. You are here to risk your heart. You are here to be swallowed up. And when it happens that you are broken, or betrayed, or left, or hurt, or death brushes near, let yourself sit by an apple tree and listen to the apples falling all around you in heaps, wasting their sweetness. Tell yourself that you tasted as many as you could.

—LOUISE ERDRICH, *The Painted Drum*

midding

n. the tranquil pleasure of being near a gathering but not quite in it—hovering on the perimeter of a campfire, talking quietly outside a party, resting your eyes in the back seat of a car listening to friends chatting up front—feeling blissfully invisible yet still fully included, safe in the knowledge that everyone is together and everyone is okay, with all the thrill of being there without the burden of having to be.

Middle English *midding*, alternate spelling of *midden*, a refuse heap that sits near a dwelling. Pronounced "*mid*-ing."

flashover

n. the moment a conversation becomes real and alive, when a spark of trust shorts out the delicate circuits you keep insulated under layers of irony, momentarily grounding the static emotional charge you've built up through decades of friction with the world.

In firefighting, a *flashover* is when all the flammable material in an area combusts all at once.

incidental contact high

n. an innocuous touch by someone just doing their job—a barber, yoga instructor, or friendly waitress—that you find more meaningful than you'd like to admit; a feeling of connection so stupefyingly simple it makes you wonder if aspiring novelists would be better off just offering people a hug.

In sports, *incidental contact* is a glancing touch that doesn't rise to the level of a foul. A *contact high* is when you feel the effects of a drug vicariously.

fensiveness

n. a knee-jerk territorial reaction when a friend displays a casual interest in one of your obsessions.

Mandarin 粉絲 (*fěnsī*), fan, admirer + *defensiveness*. Pronounced "*fen*-siv-nis."

mottleheaded

adj. feeling uneasy when socializing with odd combinations of friends and family, or friends and colleagues, or colleagues and family—mixing a medley of ingredients that don't typically go together, which risks either watering down your identity into gray mush, or accidentally triggering some sort of explosion.

From *motley*, comprising incongruous elements + *headed*. Pronounced "*mot*-l-hed-id."

the McFly effect

n. the phenomenon of observing your parents interact with people they grew up with, which reboots their personalities into youth mode, offering you a glimpse of the dreamers and rascals they used to be, before you came into the picture.

Refers to Marty McFly, the protagonist of *Back to the Future*, who travels back in time and interacts with his parents while they're still in their teens.

moledro

n. a feeling of resonant connection with an author or artist you'll never meet, who may have lived centuries ago and thousands of miles away but can still get inside your head and leave behind morsels of their experience, like the little piles of stones left by hikers that mark a hidden path through unfamiliar territory.

Portuguese *moledro*, cairn. According to Portuguese legend, if you take a stone from a cairn and put it under a pillow, in the morning an enchanted soldier will appear for a moment, before transforming back into the stone and returning to the pile. Pronounced "moh-*leh*-droh."

OPIA

the ambiguous intensity of eye contact

So much can be said in a glance. You feel such ambiguous intensity, looking someone in the eye—it's somehow both intrusive and vulnerable. Their pupils glittering black, bottomless, and opaque.

The eye is a keyhole through which the world pours in, and a world spills out. For a few seconds, you can peek through into a vault that contains everything they are. Catching a glimpse of their vulnerability, their pain, their humor, their vitality, their power over others, and what they demand of themselves. But whether the eyes are the windows of the soul or the doors of perception, it doesn't really matter: you're still standing on the outside of the house.

Eye contact isn't really contact at all. It's only ever a glance—a near-miss—that you can only feel as it slips past you. There's so much that we keep in the back room; so much that other people never get to see. We only ever offer up a sample of who we are, of what we think people want us to be. And yet, how rarely do we stop to look inside, let our eyes adjust, and try to see what's really there, the worlds hidden away in the eyes of others.

You too are peering out from behind your own door. You put yourself out there, trying to decide how much of the world to let in. It's all too easy for others to size you up and carry on their way. They can see you more clearly than you ever could. Yours is the only vault you can't see into, that you can't size up in an instant. You'll always have to wonder if someone might come along and peer into your soul. Or if anyone out there will put in the effort, trying to find the key.

We're all just exchanging glances, trying to tell each other who we are. Trying to catch a glimpse of ourselves, feeling around in the darkness.

Greek ὄπιο (ópio), opium + -ωπία (-opía), of the eyes. The word *pupil* is from the Latin *pupilla*, "little girl-doll," a reference to the tiny image of yourself you see reflected in the eyes of another. This idea was the origin of the Elizabethan expression *to look babies*, which means "to stare lovingly into another's eyes." Pronounced "*oh*-pee-uh."

hickering

n. the habit of falling hard for whatever pretty new acquaintance happens to come along, spending hours wallowing in the handful of details you can gather about them, connecting the dots into elaborate constellations, even imagining an entire future together—images that have no particular purpose, except that they're kinda fun to think about.

Hebrew וירקה (hikrín), to project an image + *hankering*, craving. Pronounced "*hik*-er-ing."

feresy

n. the fear that your partner is changing in ways you don't understand, even though they might be changes for the better, because it forces you to wonder whether your relationship needs a few careful nudges to fall back into balance, or perhaps is still as stable as ever, but involves a person who no longer exists.

Middle English *fere*, partner, companion + *heresy*, deviation from established practices or beliefs. Pronounced "*fer*-uh-see."

bye-over

n. the sheepish casual vibe between two people who've shared an emotional farewell but then unexpectedly have a little extra time together, wordlessly agreeing to pretend that they've already moved on.

From *good-bye* + *do-over*.

skidding

v. intr. the practice of making offhand comments that sound sarcastic but are actually sincere and deeply felt.

From *skidding*, going farther than intended out of inertia + *kidding*, joking around.

ochisia

n. the fear that the role you once occupied in someone's life could be refilled without a second thought, which makes you wish that every breakup would include a severance package, a non-compete clause, and some sort of romantic placement program.

Greek όχι πια (*óchi pia*), not anymore. Pronounced "oh-*kee*-zee-uh."

mornden

n. the self-contained pajama universe shared by two people on a long weekend morning, withdrawing from the world and letting the hours slow to a crawl, coming as close as they'll ever get to pausing the flow of time, even as they know it'll eventually rush back in all the faster.

From *morn*, morning + *den*, a comfortable room that affords private time. Pronounced "*mawrn*-duhn."

nachlophobia

n. the fear that your deepest connections with people are ultimately pretty shallow, that although your relationships feel congenial in the moment, an audit of your life would reveal a smattering of low-interest holdings and uninvested windfall profits, which will indicate you were never really at risk of joy, sacrifice, or loss.

Greek αναχλός (*anachlós*), loosely held together + -φοβία (*-phobía*), fear. May also appear as *apomakrysmenophobia*. Pronounced "nok-luh-*foh*-bee-uh."

fardle-din

n. a long-overdue argument that shakes up a relationship, burning wildly through your issues like a forest fire, which clears out your dry and hollow grievances and reminds you that your roots run deeper than you think.

Middle English *fardel*, burden or bundle + *din*, a loud cacophonous noise. Pronounced "*fahr*-dl-din."

dolonia

n. a state of unease prompted by people who seem to like you too much, which makes you wonder if they must have you confused with someone else—someone flawless, selfless, or easy to understand from a distance—feeling vaguely disappointed that they're unwilling to spend the time it takes getting to know the real you.

Ancient Greek εἴδωλον (*eídōlon*), a phantom image of an ideal form. Pronounced "duh-*loh*-nee-uh."

suente

n. the state of being so familiar with someone that you can be in a room with them without thinking, without holding anything back, or without having to say a word—to the extent that you have to remind yourself that they're a different being entirely, that brushing hair away from their eyes won't help you see any better.

Southwest English dialect *suent*, easy, peaceful, smooth. Pronounced "soo-*ent*-ey."

lilo

n. a friendship that can lie dormant for years only to pick right back up instantly, as if you'd seen each other last week—which is all the more remarkable given that certain other people can make every lull in conversation feel like an eternity.

From *lifelong* + *lie low*. Pronounced "*lahy*-loh."

querinous

adj. longing for a sense of certainty in a relationship; wishing there were some way to know ahead of time whether this is the person you're going to wake up next to for twenty thousand mornings in a row, instead of having to count them out one by one, quietly hoping your streak continues.

Mandarin 确认 (*quèrèn*), confirmation. Twenty thousand days is roughly fifty-five years. Pronounced "*kweh*-ruh-nuhs."

watashiato

n. curiosity about the impact you've had on the lives of the people you know, wondering which of your harmless actions or long-forgotten words might have altered the plot of their stories in ways you'll never get to see.

Japanese 私 (*watashi*), I + 足跡 (*ashiato*), footprint. Pronounced "wah-tah-shee-*ah*-toh."

fata organa

n. a flash of real emotion glimpsed in someone sitting across the room—their mind wandering away from whatever's happening around them, their eyes lighting up with pensiveness or vulnerability or cosmic boredom—as if you could see backstage through a gap in the curtains, watching actors in costume mouthing their lines, fragments of bizarre sets waiting for some other production.

From *fata morgana*, a kind of mirage that warps the appearance of distant objects so that sailboats look like fairy castles + *organa*, methods by which a philosophical investigation may be conducted. Pronounced "*fah*-tuh awr-*gah*-nuh."

amoransia

n. the melodramatic thrill of unrequited love; the longing to pine for someone you can never have, wallowing in devotion to some impossible person who could give your life meaning by their very absence.

Portuguese *amor*, love + *ânsia*, craving. Pronounced "ah-moh-*ran*-see-uh."

redesis

n. a feeling of queasiness while offering someone advice, knowing they might well face a totally different set of constraints and capabilities, any of which might propel them to a wildly different outcome—which makes you wonder if all of your hard-earned wisdom is fundamentally nontransferable, like handing someone a gift card in your name that probably expired years ago.

Middle English *rede*, advice + *pedesis*, the random motion of particles. Pronounced "ruh-*dee*-sis."

Fig. 6. Moment of Tangency. | Collage by Sammy Slabbinck | sammyslabbinck.com

MOMENT OF TANGENCY

*a fleeting glimpse of
what might have been*

You and I have never met, many times before. Our paths might have crossed once or twice online, or while passing in the street. We might have spent an hour sitting back-to-back at the same airport gate, or even exchanged a few words over the phone, when I dialed your number by mistake. For all we know, we might have been living in the same neighborhood for decades—but against incredible odds, we just happened to miss each other. It's a big world, after all.

Our days must be filled with these chance encounters, that for a million tiny reasons, never actually happen. Our streets must be teeming with accidental strangers, who just happened to miss their cue—who share everything in common, except for time and place. For years, their stories might've been happening in parallel, harmonizing from somewhere across the world, but neither has any idea that the other even exists. If two lines are truly parallel, it means they'll never actually meet.

It's hard not to think of your own near-misses, veering away on a tangent in some alternate universe. The person who would've been your best friend in the world might be out there somewhere, milling around a party you weren't invited to. Your business partner might be sitting on half of a world-changing idea, waiting for your contribution to arrive, though it never will. It's hard not to glance at a stranger in a crowd and imagine the life you might have shared, if only things had been different—feeling a pang of missed connection as you carry on your separate ways, leaving nothing but an echo of something that might have been.

You never know how many things had to happen exactly right for you to meet the one you love. You never know how easily fate might have tipped you onto some other course, meeting some stranger, who might have felt like a soulmate. As you sit there on your commuter train, wrapped up in your own concerns, you have no way of knowing how close you're sitting to the person you might have loved, who you might have spent years with, even built a family. You would have looked across the room at this same face, and struggled to imagine life without them, telling yourself that it was always meant to be. As if you had known all along that your paths would cross eventually.

Maybe you were always destined to be sitting right where you're sitting. Or maybe it's a miracle that you managed to meet the people you did, knowing how many obstacles might have gotten in the way. Or maybe it's nothing personal, and it was all just a coincidence. You never know.

In geometry, a *tangent* is the point at which a line "just touches" a curve, where they share precisely the same angle, before separating again and carrying on to infinity.

waldosia

n. a condition in which you keep scanning faces in a crowd looking for a specific person who would have no reason to be there, as if your brain is checking to see whether they're still in your life, subconsciously patting its emotional pockets before it leaves for the day.

From the *Where's Waldo?* series of picture books, or in some countries, *Where's Wally?*, in which the reader tries to spot one specific person somewhere in a massive crowd. Pronounced "wawl-*doh*-zhuh" or "wawl-*doh*-see-uh."

zverism

n. the wish that people could suspend their civility and indulge the physical side of each other first—sniffing each other's hair like dogs, staring unabashedly at interesting faces, reveling in a beautiful voice like a song on the radio.

Lithuanian *žvėris*, wild beast + Latin *vērissimus*, the truest, the realest. Pronounced "*zvair*-iz-uhm."

immerensis

n. the maddening inability to understand the reasons why someone loves you—almost as if you're selling them a used car that you know has a ton of problems and requires daily tinkering just to get it to run normally, but no matter how much you try to warn them, they seem all the more eager to hop behind the wheel and see where this puppy can go.

Latin *immerens*, undeserving. Pronounced "ih-muhr-*en*-sis."

lookaback

n. the shock of meeting back up with someone and learning that your mental image of them had fallen wildly out of date—having grown up or gotten old, fallen apart or pulled themselves together—which shakes your faith in the accuracy of the social puppet show that runs continuously inside your head.

From *look back* + *taken aback*, taken by surprise.

falesia

n. the disquieting awareness that someone's importance to you and your importance to them may not necessarily match—that your best friend might only think of you as a buddy, that someone you barely know might consider you a mentor, that someone you love unconditionally might have one or two conditions.

Portuguese *falésia*, cliff. A cliff is a dizzying meeting point between high ground and low ground. Pronounced "fuh-*lee*-zhuh."

lackout

n. the sudden awareness that you're finally over someone, noticing that the same voice that once triggered a cocktail of emotions now evokes nothing at all—as if your brain had returned the last box of their things and your heart had quietly changed its locks.

From *lack*, missing something + *blackout*, when a spark abruptly goes away.

rivener

n. a chilling hint of distance that creeps slowly into a relationship—beginning to notice them laugh a little less, look away a little more, explain away their mood like it's no longer your business—as if you're watching them fall out of love right in front of you, gradually and painfully, like a hole in the radiator that leaves your house a little colder with every passing day, whose only clue is a slow, unnerving *drip—drip—drip*.

Middle English *riven*, to rend, to cleave apart. Pronounced "*riv*-uh-ner."

anderance

n. the awareness that your partner perceives the relationship from a totally different angle than you—spending years looking at a different face across the table, listening for cues in a different voice—an odd reminder that no matter how much you have in common, you're still in love with different people.

Dutch *ander*, another person, someone else. Pronounced "*an*-der-uhns."

ecstatic shock

n. a surge of energy upon catching a glance from someone you like, which scrambles your ungrounded circuits and tempts you to chase after that feeling with a kite and a key.

From *ecstatic*, deliriously happy + *static shock*, a charge of potential energy that builds up invisibly until it sparks across the air.

foilsick

adj. feeling ashamed after revealing a little too much of yourself to someone—allowing them too clear a view of your pettiness, your anger, your cowardice, your childlike vulnerability—wishing you could somehow take back the moment, discreetly bolting the door after a storm had already blown it off its hinges.

Scottish Gaelic *foillsich*, to expose.

AMICY

the mystery of what goes on
behind the scenes of your social life

It's comforting to imagine that conspiracies run our world. To think there is some hidden order to things, a superstructure held high over our heads by a shadowy cabal of insiders. Of course, there's no hidden order—but then again, of course there is. It's all of us. We're all insiders, managing an intricate web of relationships, deploying hundreds of unseen gestures and soft power plays, soaking up gossip with all the urgency of counterintelligence. It's at once mundane, and yet no less chilling than any other conspiracy, because it leaves you questioning the very fabric of reality, wondering what you don't know.

Ask yourself—how many cover-ups have you taken part in? How many times have you heard something you weren't supposed to hear, withheld certain details to make your case, deftly changed the subject, or tried to steer someone's behavior without them knowing? If you can do all that without a second thought, everyone around you must be doing it, too.

Of course, you'd like to think you've got a clear view of the broader social landscape, but it's possible you don't have a clue. There are so many backstories that people keep to themselves, so many back channels you don't even know exist. Random clusters of friends might be carrying on parallel conversations in another group text, or meeting up regularly at events you're not invited to. People know far more about you than you think, holding on to secrets and rumors they use to inform your character but never mention in your presence. Some of your friends are vastly different people when they're one-on-one with each other, such that both would seem unrecognizable. Even now an unexpected pair of them might be helping each other through a crisis, or carrying on a silent feud, or having a fling that you won't hear about until years later. There might be a big dramatic event going on that bends the course of our lives, except for certain people left out of the loop, who'll always have to wonder. And even if everything was open and honest, you'd still have to confront the ever-shifting labyrinth of interconnected relationships and personas and levels of intimacy you could scarcely even begin to fathom.

It's enough to make you crazy, never knowing if you're living in an alternate reality being constructed around you. But perhaps there's some comfort in that uncertainty. After all, cui bono? Who benefits? For all you know, it might be you. Who knows how many colleagues called in favors to get you an interview or lobbied hard to save your job? How many little crises were happening on your wedding day that were deliberately hidden from your view? Protectors all around you might be sheltering you from looming dangers, so you never have to lose sleep knowing how at risk you really were. Your family might spend hours discussing where your life is going, comparing notes to figure out what you need the most right now. Sometimes your friends will wait until you leave the table before they all start singing your praises, only to change the subject just before you return. It's not a crazy thought. It happens all the time.

None of us knows the full picture of what's really going on. All we know for sure is that some mysterious force is working behind the scenes to keep our communities intact and our relationships running—sometimes smoothly, sometimes not. But we all sleep a little better, knowing some sort of conspiracy is afoot. Otherwise we'd be tossing and turning all night, haunted by the notion that we're all just acting alone.

From *amity*, friendship + *conspiracy*, a collective plot to secretly pursue a sinister goal. Pronounced "*am*-uh-see."

dead reckoning

v. intr. finding yourself bothered by somebody's death more than you would have expected, even if they were only an abstract presence in your life, like a lighthouse in the distance that suddenly goes dark, leaving you with one less landmark to navigate by.

In navigation, *dead reckoning* is the practice of using your prior course to extrapolate your subsequent position. It can be useful on starless nights but often leads to cumulative errors; if you don't often check your position against new data, you might end up completely lost.

etherness

n. the wistful feeling of looking around a gathering of loved ones, all too aware that even though the room is filled with warmth and laughter now, it won't always be this way—that the coming years will steadily break people away into their own families, or see them pass away one by one, until there comes a time when you'll look back and try to imagine what it felt like to have everyone together in the same place.

From *ether*, an intoxicating compound that evaporates very quickly + *togetherness*. Pronounced "*eth*-er-nis."

fawtle

n. a weird little flaw built into your partner that some-how only endears them more to you, in the way that im-purities dissolved in water are what allow it to conduct electricity—if all the imperfections were removed, there would be no spark.

Middle English *fawteles*, without a defect. Pronounced "*faw*-tuhl."

dolorblindness

n. the frustration that you'll never be able to understand another person's pain, only ever searching their face for some faint evocation of it, then rifling through your own experiences for some slapdash comparison, wishing you could tell them truthfully, "I know exactly how you feel."

Latin *dolor*, pain + *colorblindness*. Pronounced "*doh*-ler-blahynd-nis."

on tenderhooks

adj. feeling the primal satisfaction of being needed by someone, which makes you feel that much more rooted to the world, even if the roots belong to someone else.

From *tender*, emotionally raw + *hooks*, a tool for binding one thing to another. Compare *on tenterhooks*, which is a state of anxious suspense.

los vidados

n. the half-remembered acquaintances you knew years ago, who you might have forgotten completely if someone hadn't happened to mention them again—friends of friends, people you once shared classes with, people you heard stories about, who you didn't know well but who still made up the fabric of your intense little community—making you wonder who else might be out there somewhere, only just remembering that you exist.

Spanish *los olvidados*, "the forgotten"—but not completely. Pronounced "lohs vee-*dah*-dohs."

soufrise

n. the maddening thrill of an ambiguous flirtation, which quivers in tension halfway between platonic and romantic—*maybe, but no, but maybe*—leaving you guessing what's going on inside their chest, forced to assume that at any given moment their attraction is both alive and dead at the same time.

French *sourire*, smile + *frisson*, a shiver of chill or excitement. Pronounced "soo-*freez*."

the kinder surprise

n. the point in your early adolescence when you realize that your parents are muddling through their lives the same as you; that many respectable adults are no less lost than you and your friends, no less petty and obsessive and insecure, which makes you wonder if there are no real adults, because such a thing never actually existed, except in bedtime stories.

German *Kinder*, children. Refers to *Kinder Surprise*, a foil-wrapped chocolate egg that contains a small toy that's already broken into pieces. Pronounced "thuh *kin*-der ser-*prahyz*."

la gaudière

n. a glint of goodness you notice in someone that you wouldn't expect, which is often only detectable by sloshing them back and forth in your mind until everything dark and gray and common falls away, leaving something shining at the bottom of the pan—a rare element hidden deep in the bedrock, that must've been washed there by a storm somewhere upstream.

French *la gaudière*, from Latin *gaudere*, to find joy. Pronounced "lah gou-dee-*yair*."

attriage

n. the state of having lost all control over how you feel about someone—not even trying to quench the flames anymore, but lighting other fires around your head just hoping to contain the damage.

From *atria*, the chambers of the heart + *triage*, the sorting of patients in hospital admissions, factoring in the urgency of their illness or injury. Pronounced "at-ree-*ahzh*."

mauerbauertraurigkeit

n. the inexplicable urge to push people away, even close friends whose company you generally enjoy—like a poker player who keeps folding a promising hand in order to avoid the pain of losing, or tamp down the urge to go all-in.

German *Mauerbauer*, wall-builder + *Traurigkeit*, sadness. Pronounced "mou-er-bou-er-*trou*-rikh-kahyt."

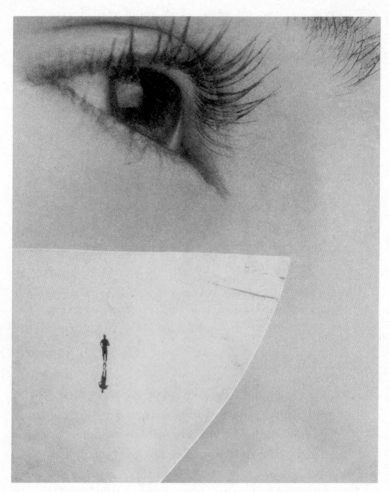

Fig. 7. Gnossienne. | Collage by Elsa Leone | Instagram @elsabottingleone

GNOSSIENNE

*the awareness that someone you've known for years
still has a private and mysterious inner life*

It's a joy to get to know someone over the course of many years. Learning her secrets, the color of her humor, the precise vibration of the mind-gears turning inside her skull. But sometimes you look across the room and catch a glimpse of her just being herself—brushing her teeth, or chatting away at a dinner party, or telling you about her day—and even though you may have seen her do it thousands of times, you begin to look at her in a different light, struck by her sheer uniqueness. Nobody else knows her in the same way you do. There's only one of her in the universe. And here she is.

You take in the details of her face and try to imagine what you'd think if you didn't know her name, if she were just some stranger on the street. It makes her seem ennobled in a way—a mortal being with a heartbeat, infused with a pathos and humor and a vulnerability you've never noticed before. For a moment you're able to strip away the baggage of what she is to you and the roles she plays in your life. It's easy to forget that she doesn't just exist in the contexts you tend to see her in, not just one half of a couple, or one ingredient in a broader social soup, but steeped in her own unique vibe wherever she goes. Around her are a menagerie of relationships with hundreds of people you'll never meet. Whatever she is to you, to them she might be a wildly different figure: an intimidating boss, a childhood buddy, the comic relief, or the one who got away.

And when she's alone, she's someone else entirely, a person you'll never get a chance to meet. You can imagine her looking over her reflection in the bathroom mirror, making goofy faces, or reminding herself to live in the moment, to be herself, to get through the day. While falling asleep at night, she might be thinking over the parts of herself that make her feel proud, or self-conscious, or ashamed, trying to be a better person, even questioning the very traits that you love most about her. She might be going back through her memories, sifting through fragments and echoes, curating an entire alternate history that she keeps locked away from you: remnants of another life. Every word she speaks is thrumming with emotional resonances you can't hear, informed by a context she'll never be able to explain. She has desires too raw to defend, fears she can't bear to think about. And all of this is happening all the time, invisibly, right there in front of you.

You'll never fully know her, not really. As long as she lives, she'll never find the right words to truly convey what goes on inside her head. But if it's any consolation, she'll never know you either. There will always be this fundamental separation between you. People sometimes speak of a relationship as a kind of union, but in truth, you are two separate people, with different lives, different bodies, a different past, and a different future. Each of you is a wholeness unto itself, with a tiny but unmistakable gap.

And yet, by some miracle, you're able to transcend that separation. Over the course of years spent together, sharing your lives side by side, you feel something begin to take shape in the air between you, some third thing that takes on a life of its own. It's like putting two images together and flickering them back and forth until they appear to spring into motion, infused with a life that wasn't there in either one alone. When the interplay between you slows too much, the illusion is broken, and you recall your separateness. The best you can do is try to keep it going, keeping up the rhythm of all the little daily gestures and exchanges, the call-and-response of daily life, and hope it all works out.

There will always be a certain distance between us. Maybe the cynics are right, and love is only ever an illusion. But maybe it's the sacred kind of illusion, like the shimmering blue gods who appear to shepherd children. It has power, if only because we believe it does. And that's enough. All that is required is that we keep showing up, and never stop asking each other, "What are you thinking about?"

It's not about getting an answer to the question. It's the act of asking, of trying to reach across the gap, working through the mystery—that is what's worth holding on to.

That's the feeling that must be kept alive, even if we never find the right words to express it.

Borrowed from the title of a piano composition by Erik Satie; its etymology is a mystery but may refer to Greek *gnosis*, knowledge, or *Knossos*, the mythical setting of the Minotaur and the labyrinth. Pronounced "nos-*yen*."

dorgone

adj. wondering if you could slip away from an event or group conversation without anyone noticing your absence.

Old Norse *dár*, benumbed + *forgone*, to have already left or abstained. Pronounced "dohr-*gon*."

semaphorism

n. a conversational hint that you have something personal to say on the subject but don't go any further—an emphatic nod, a half-told anecdote, an enigmatic "I know the feeling"—which you place into conversations like those little flags that warn diggers of something buried underground: an unexploded bomb, a sacred burial ground, or a high-voltage cable that secretly powers your house.

From *semaphore*, a communication method used at sea, in which sailors stand on deck and move flags into certain positions to convey simple messages. Pronounced "sem-uh-*fawr*-iz-uhm."

drisson

> *n.* an unexpected twinge of attraction for a friend; a flutter of desire you don't necessarily want to feel, that didn't even seem possible up until this point, when it suddenly becomes a problem you have to deal with.

From *frisson*, a shiver of excitement + *dribber*, an inaccurate archer. Pronounced "dree-*sawn*."

sitheless

> *adj.* feeling wistful upon brushing past a person you once shared a life with—noticing the same touch on the arm, seeing the same smile, hearing the same laugh you used to adore—suddenly all too aware that it's no longer for you, and no longer carries the meaning it once did.

Old English *sithen*, since then + *natheless*, not less by that. Pronounced "*sih*-thuh-les."

hubilance

> *n.* the quiet poignance of your own responsibility for someone, with a mix of pride and fear and love and humility—feeling a baby fall asleep on your chest, or driving at night surrounded by loved ones fast asleep, who trust you implicitly with their lives—a responsibility that

wasn't talked about or assigned to you, it was assumed to be yours without question.

From *hub*, the central part of the wheel that bears the weight + *jubilance*. Pronounced "*hyoo*-buh-luhns."

thrapt

adj. awed at the impact someone has had on your life, feeling intimidated by how profoundly they helped shape your identity, having served as a ghostwriter of a work that nevertheless only appears under your name.

From *thrapped*, drawn tight, as with nautical ropes + *rapt*, carried away with emotion.

heartworm

n. a relationship or friendship that you can't get out of your head, which you thought had faded long ago but is still somehow alive and unfinished, like an abandoned campsite whose smoldering embers still have the power to start a forest fire.

From *heart* + *earworm*, a catchy piece of music that compulsively loops inside your head.

antiophobia

n. a fear you sometimes experience while leaving a loved one, wondering if this will turn out to be the last time you'll ever see them, and whatever slapdash good-bye you toss their way might have to serve as your final farewell.

Greek αντίο (*antío*), farewell + -φοβία (*-phobía*), fear. Pronounced "an-tee-uh-*foh*-bee-uh."

hanker sore

adj. finding a person so attractive it actually kinda pisses you off.

From *hanker*, to pine after something + *canker sore*, which gets worse the more you're aware of it.

FOUR

Faces in a Crowd

CATCHING GLIMPSES OF
HUMANITY FROM A DISTANCE

Collage by Robyn Redish | Instagram @stolenpainting

We all have our little solipsistic delusions, ghastly intuitions of utter singularity: that we are the only one in the house who ever fills the ice-cube tray, who unloads the clean dishwasher, who occasionally pees in the shower, whose eyelid twitches on first dates; that only we take casualness terribly seriously; that only we fashion supplication into courtesy; that only we hear the whiny pathos in a dog's yawn, the timeless sigh in the opening of the hermetically-sealed jar, the splattered laugh in the frying egg, the minor-D lament in the vacuum's scream; that only we feel the panic at sunset the rookie kindergartner feels at his mother's retreat. That only we love the only-we. That only we need the only-we. Solipsism binds us together. . . . That we feel lonely in a crowd; stop not to dwell on what's brought the crowd into being. That we are, always, faces in a crowd.

—DAVID FOSTER WALLACE,
Girl with Curious Hair

Fig. 8. Sonder. | Collage by John Koenig | dictionaryofobscuresorrows.com

SONDER

the awareness that everyone has a story

You are the main character. The protagonist. The star at the center of your own unfolding story. You're surrounded by your supporting cast: friends and family hanging in your immediate orbit. Scattered a little further out, a network of acquaintances who drift in and out of contact over the years.

But there in the background, faint and out of focus, are the extras. The random passersby. Each living a life as vivid and complex as your own. They carry on invisibly around you, bearing the accumulated weight of their own ambitions, friends, routines, mistakes, worries, triumphs, and inherited craziness.

When your life moves on to the next scene, theirs flickers in place, wrapped in a cloud of backstory and inside jokes and characters strung together with countless other stories you'll never be able to see. That you'll never know exist. In which you might appear only once. As an extra sipping coffee in the background. As a blur of traffic passing on the highway. As a lighted window at dusk.

French *sonder*, to plumb the depths. Pronounced "*sahn*-der." Can be used as a noun or a verb, as you would use the word *wonder*.

hailbound

adj. mysteriously compelled to wave to passing strangers on a country road, a mountain path, or a remote stretch of water.

From *hail*, to greet + *bound*, being obliged.

monachopsis

n. the subtle but persistent feeling of being out of place, as maladapted to your surroundings as a seal on a beach, lumbering and clumsy, huddled in the company of other misfits, dreaming of life in your natural habitat, a place where you'd be fluidly, brilliantly, effortlessly at home.

Ancient Greek μοναχός (*monakhós*), single, solitary + ὄψις (*ópsis*), vision. Pronounced "mon-uh-*kop*-sis."

kenaway

n. the longing to see how other people live their lives when they're not in public; wishing you could tune in to the raw feed of another human existence, in all its messiness and solitude—shimmying in place while brushing their teeth, squabbling over where to put the shoes, talking out their problems on solitary commutes—if only to give you something to compare your own life against, and figure out whether you're bizarrely normal or normally bizarre.

From *ken*, one's range of knowledge + *keep-away*, a game in which one player tries to intercept a ball being tossed back and forth by two others. Pronounced "*ken*-uh-wey."

ludiosis

n. the sense that you're just making it up as you go along—knowing that if someone asked why you do most things, you couldn't really come up with a convincing explanation.

In Ancient Rome, *Ludi Osci*, the Oscan Games, gave rise to the art of improvisational theater. Pronounced "loo-dee-*oh*-sis."

routwash

n. a moment of panic that you'll end up looking back on years of labor with little to show for it, that despite all the time you've spent gathering skills and connections and experiences, many of them will prove to have been worth almost nothing in the long run, redeemable for petty cash, a line on a résumé, a few compliments, or a handful of magic beans.

From *rout*, a chaotic retreat + *wash*, a meager return on investment + *outwash*, the gravelly sediment left by water flowing from a melting glacier.

eisce

n. the awareness of the infinitesimal role you play in shaping your own society—knowing that whenever you smile at a stranger, pronounce a word a certain way, laugh at a certain joke, or choose the slightly shinier apple, you are unwittingly helping to construct the world in which you live—a role both vanishingly small but also somehow daunting, making it that much harder to complain about the traffic, knowing that you are traffic.

Irish *eisceacht*, exception. Pronounced "*ahy*-shuh."

kuebiko

n. a state of exhaustion inspired by senseless tragedies and acts of violence, which force you to abruptly revise your expectations of what can happen in this world, trying to prop yourself up like an old scarecrow, who's bursting at the seams yet powerless to do anything but stand there and watch.

In Japanese mythology, *Kuebiko* is the name of a kami deity, a scarecrow who stands all day watching the world go by, which has made him very wise but locked in place. Pronounced "koo-*web*-i-koh."

lockheartedness

n. the atmosphere of camaraderie when people are stuck together in a certain place—a stalled elevator, a shelter during a storm, the sleeper car of a train—which leaves them no other option but to be present with each other, with nowhere else to go, and nobody else to be.

From *locked up* + *fullheartedness*.

LUMUS

*the poignant humanness
beneath the spectacle of society*

Your culture never really leaves you. Its rhythms are encoded in your heartbeat, its music embedded in the sound of your voice. Its images make up the raw material of your wildest dreams, your deepest fears, even your attempts to rebel against it. So it's hard not to get swept up in the spectacle of it all, absorbing its stories and values and symbols until you no longer question their importance. It's as if there's a circus whirling around you all the time, so overwhelming that you keep forgetting it's there.

But there are still moments when you manage to tune out the fanfare—taking time in nature, in solitude, or in some other culture entirely—getting away long enough so that when you return to normal life again, you're able to look around with fresh eyes, and see how abnormal it really is.

You take in all the scenes and sideshows happening around you. It doesn't quite feel like reality anymore, more like the worldbuilding of a fantasy novel. You have no idea who came up with this stuff, but you can't help but be impressed by their tireless dedication to fleshing out even the most mundane details. The vaunted marble halls of politics and business and religion and the arts, each buttressed by its own rules and standards and practices, booming with the echoes of a billion conversations that everyone seems to take so very seriously. Rituals of status and fashion, the mythology of the markets, pop-culture think pieces, and waves upon waves of breaking news. You wonder how you ever managed to get so invested, following all these stock characters, and all their little dramas and debates. Who said what to whom? What does it all mean? What will happen next?

You're struck by how arbitrary and provisional it all feels. Though it has all the weight of reality, you know it could just as easily have been something else. You realize that all of our big ideas and sacred institutions were designed and built by ordinary human beings, soft-bellied mammals, who shiver when they're cold, dance around when they have to pee, and lash out when they feel powerless. So much of our culture exists because someone was hungry once, someone was bored, someone was afraid, someone wanted to impress a mate, prove someone wrong, or leave their kids a better life.

The circus is so big and bright and loud, it's easy to believe that that's the real world and you live somewhere outside it. But beneath all these constructed ideals, there is a darker heart of normalcy, a humble humanness, that powers the whole thing. We're all just people. We go to work and play our roles as best we can, spinning our tales and performing our tricks, but then we take off our makeup and go home, where we carry on with our real lives. None of us really knows what is happening, what we're doing, where we're going, or why. Still we carry on, doing what we can to get through it. Even the roar of the city can sometimes feel like a cry for help.

Inevitably, within a few days or weeks at most, you'll find yourself getting swept right back into the big show, even though you know it's all just an act. That's perhaps the most amazing thing about a society: even if none of us fully believes in it, we're all willing to come together and pretend we do, doing our part to hold up the tent. If only so we can shut out the darkness for a little while, and offer each other the luxury of thinking that little things matter a great deal.

We know it's all so silly and meaningless, and yet we're still here, holding our breath together, waiting to see what happens next. And tomorrow, we'll put ourselves out there and do it all again. The show must go on.

Latin *lumen*, light, brightness + *humus*, a particularly rich and dark component of soil, made of decayed organic matter. Pronounced "*loo*-muhs."

catoptric tristesse

n. the sadness that you'll never really know what other people think of you, whether good, bad, or if at all—that although you can gather a few hints here and there, and even ask around for honest feedback, you'll always have to wonder which opinions are being softened out of flattery, sharpened out of malice, or held back because it's simply not their place.

In Ancient Rome, the *catoptric cistula* was a kind of mirror-lined box whose interior appeared to expand into an infinite forest, library, or treasure room. Pronounced "kuh-*top*-trik tris-*tes*."

pax latrina

n. the meditative atmosphere of being alone in a bathroom, sequestered inside your own little isolation booth, enjoying a moment backstage from the razzle-dazzle of public life.

Latin *pax*, a period of peace + *latrina*, toilet. Compare *Pax Romana* or *Pax Americana*; sometimes the solace of bathroom stalls can feel just as profound as the protection of empires. Pronounced "paks luh-*tree*-nah."

wytai

n. a feature of modern civilization that suddenly strikes you as absurd and grotesque—from pets and milk drinking to organ transplants, life insurance, and fiction—part of a rich legacy of absurdity that dates all the way back to the moment our ancestors first hauled themselves out of the slime, but could not for the life of them remember what they got up to do.

Acronym of When You Think About It. Pronounced "*wahy*-tahy."

burn upon reentry

n. the bitter disappointment upon finding no new messages after spending hours out of contact, as if the world had barely even noticed you had left.

From the tendency of spacefaring objects to heat up upon reentering the atmosphere.

anecdoche

n. a conversation in which everyone is talking but nobody is listening—instead merely overlaying words like a spoken game of Scrabble, each player borrowing bits of others' anecdotes to build out their own, until we reach a point when we all run out of things to say.

From *anecdote*, a short and often amusing account of real-life events + *synecdoche*, a figure of speech in which a part stands for the whole. Pronounced "uh-*nek*-doh-kee."

xeno

n. the smallest measurable unit of human connection, typically exchanged between passing strangers—a warm smile, a sympathetic nod, a shared laugh about some odd coincidence—moments that are fleeting and random but still contain powerful emotional nutrients that can alleviate the symptoms of feeling alone.

Ancient Greek ξένος (*xénos*), alien, stranger. Pronounced "*zee*-noh."

amuse-douche

n. an activity that you've adored since you were a kid—riding bikes, reading books, taking pictures, cooking food—whose enjoyment dissolves on contact with hardcore fanatics' ferocious obsession with technique.

From *amuse-bouche*, a bite-size appetizer intended to tantalize the palate + *douche*. Pronounced "ah-mooz-*doosh*."

pâro

n. the feeling that everything you do is always somehow wrong—that there's nothing you can eat that's actually healthy, nothing you can say that isn't problematic, no way to raise your kids that won't leave them traumatized—which makes you wonder if there's some obvious way forward that everybody can see but you, each of them leaning back in their chair and calling out helpfully, "Colder . . . colder . . . colder . . ."

From *par 0* (*par zero*), a theoretical hole on a golf course in which it's already too late—no matter how well you hit the ball, you've already fallen behind. The circumflex on the *â* is a tiny symbol of someone trying for something then retreating. Compare the Spanish *paro,* a stoppage or a freezing-up. Pronounced "*pahr*-oh."

adronitis

n. frustration with how long it takes to get to know someone—spending the first few weeks chatting in their psychological entryway, with each subsequent conversation like entering a different anteroom, each a little closer to the center of the house—wishing instead that you could start there and work your way out, exchanging your deepest secrets first, before easing into casualness, until you've built up enough mystery over the years to ask them where they're from and what they do for a living.

In Ancient Roman architecture, an *andronitis* is a hallway connecting the front part of the house with a complex inner atrium. One quirk of Roman houses is that all the rooms in the front have Greek names, but all the back rooms are in Latin—as if your outer self and your inner self are speaking in completely different languages. Pronounced "ad-roh-*nahy*-tis."

Fig. 9. Socha. | Collage by Alex Eckman-Lawn | alexeckmanlawn.com

SOCHA

the hidden vulnerability of others

There's an optical illusion that's easy to fall for, even if you know the trick: the more distant you are from other people, the more invulnerable they appear.

You see yourself as you are, with your failures just as clear as your successes. But you see most other people on their terms—only from the side they want you to see, like a statue on a high pedestal, stoic and confident. At first glance, they've got everything figured out, with every feature set in stone, exactly as they had intended. They appear securely embedded in their community, wrapped up tightly with their loved ones. Their life seems complete, like a finished work of art.

But it's only just a trick of perspective, because you can't see the cracks from so far away. You have no way of knowing how insecure their footing might be, how malleable they really are. How many years of effort might've gone into shaping their persona into something acceptable. How many hands it takes just to get them through an ordinary day, and keep them from falling to pieces.

Each of us is only ever a work in progress; we all have weaknesses we're not sure how to fix. So why does it feel so surprising when we catch a glimpse of vulnerability in others? Why do we keep falling for the same old trick, when each of us spends so much time trying to get away with it ourselves? Who knows why we harbor such public confidence and such private doubts?

Maybe we need to think of others as statues, and ourselves as fragile blobs of clay. Maybe that contradiction is what keeps us moving, wanting to better ourselves, and be more than what we are. Maybe it helps us keep our distance, to avoid too much friction as we brush past one another, trying to ignore how much damage we can do along the way.

Or maybe our secret vulnerability is what draws us together. It gives each of us a primal need that only a friend can satisfy—someone you trust enough to be yourself with, who can help prop you up if needed, or remind you that you're fine the way you are. And even if you're not, that's okay, too. Nothing is set in stone.

Czech *socha*, statue. Pronounced "*soh*-khuh."

tillid

adj. humbled by how readily you place your life into the hands of random strangers, often without a second thought—trusting a restaurant to check its expiration dates, trusting a construction crew not to cheap out on materials, trusting thousands of other drivers to stay in their lane—people who you may never meet but whose well-being you're deeply invested in, whether you know it or not.

Danish *tillid*, trust. Pronounced "*til*-id."

momophobia

n. the fear of speaking off the cuff or from the heart; the terror of saying the wrong thing and having to watch someone's smile fade as they realize you're not who they thought you were.

Ancient Greek μῶμος (*momos*), blemish, disgrace + -φοβία (*-phobía*), fear. Momus was the Ancient Greek god of mockery and harsh criticism. Pronounced "moh-muh-*foh*-bee-uh."

siso

n. a solitary experience you wish you could have shared with someone else—having dinner in a romantic setting, reaching the summit after an arduous climb, having a run-in with a crazy stranger that nobody's going to believe—which makes you look around for confirmation that it even happened at all.

Welsh *si-so*, see-saw, an invention that can only ever be enjoyed by multiple people; when used alone, it's just a wonky bench. Pronounced "*see*-soh."

anechosis

n. a state of exhaustion with continually being told what you want to hear, whether by marketers pandering to you or acquaintances afraid of causing offense; the longing for someone to have the heart to finally call you out on your bullshit, challenge your long-held assumptions, and push you to become a better person—which would be a far deeper kindness than trying to live and let live.

From *an-*, against + *echoes*. Pronounced "an-uh-*koh*-sis."

covalent bond

n. a moment of sudden involvement in a stranger's personal life—rushing over to break up a fight, helping a teary-eyed parent struggling with a stroller, righting someone's bike after a bad fall—that shatters the invisible glass box that usually surrounds us in public, the one we prefer to pretend is impenetrable, which somehow renders us unable to speak.

From *covalence*, literally "shared strength." In chemistry, a *covalent bond* describes the force that holds two atoms together upon sharing a loose outer shell of electron pairs. Pronounced "ko-*vey*-luhnt bond."

anaphasia

n. the fear that your society is breaking apart into factions that have nothing left in common with each other—each defending their own set of values, referring to their own cult figures, speaking in their own untranslatable language.

From *anaphase*, the stage in cell division when sister chromatids are pulled apart to opposite sides of the cell + *aphasia*, the inability to comprehend or formulate language due to brain dysfunction. Pronounced "an-uh-*fey*-zhah."

Eigenschauung

n. the degree to which your view of the world is warped by your own presence in it, whether you're a stunning beauty who assumes all strangers are chatty, a bully who thinks the world is perpetually at war, or a quivering leaf who walks around in an artificial cloud of deference; the awareness that although you'd like to think you perceive things cleanly and objectively, you've never felt the vibe of a room that doesn't happen to have you in it.

German *eigen*, inherent + *Anschauung*, view. Compare *Weltanschauung*, "worldview." Your *Weltanschauung* is how you see the world; your *Eigenschauung* is a reflection of how the world sees you. Pronounced "*ahy*-guhn-shou-oong."

ledsome

adj. feeling lonely in a crowd; drifting along in a sea of anonymous faces but unable to communicate with or confide in any of them.

Middle English *leed*, countrymen, compatriots + *lonesome.*

nullness

n. a state of instinctive restlessness that arises when your society makes too many choices on your behalf— foreclosing all risks, codifying all moral dilemmas, deciding in advance whether you'll succeed or fail—as if your conscience had been outsourced to an external provider, so it's no longer necessary to have one on site.

From *null*, an empty set of values.

holiette

n. a place that seems to hold profound significance to everyone else but you—the sacred temple of some other faith, a random fence post festooned with flowers, a crowd cheering for a team you've never heard of—which leaves you trying to coax yourself into feeling something anyway, like inserting your house key into a random lock just to feel if something clicks.

From *holy*, sacred or religiously revered + *-ette*, denoting an imitation of the real thing. Pronounced "hoh-lee-*et*."

allope

n. a mysterious aura of loneliness you feel in certain places; the palpable weight of all the lonely people secretly holed up in their houses and apartments, with a flickering blue glow cast up on their walls—so many of whom might just want someone to talk to, or just want to feel needed, and could be that for each other if only they could somehow connect.

Short for "All the lonely people," from the song "Eleanor Rigby" by the Beatles. Pronounced "*al*-uh-pee."

SILIENCE

the brilliant artistry hidden all around you

It's fun to think of your favorite musicians, back when they were just starting out. Setting up to perform on a street corner, at a time when nobody had any idea who they were. It makes you wonder: If you had been there, passing on the sidewalk as they played an early masterpiece, would you have noticed? Would you have stopped to listen?

How strange that something so vibrant as art is so nearly invisible. Strange how rarely we look up at the architecture, or savor each bite of a meal cooked with care, or stop to pay attention to the music playing in the background, that's far better than it has any right to be. It's only after someone points it out, that you finally catch the tune.

It makes you wonder if there's brilliance all around you, hiding in plain sight, just waiting around to see if you'll notice. Who knows how many Van Goghs you might be walking past, busy doing their work, just a few years too early to recognize? Maybe the next Emily Dickinson is living just down the street, sitting on an unpublished masterpiece; maybe she doesn't even suspect it, any more than we do.

We assume that if a piece is any good, surely it'll find an audience. But maybe it's mostly luck. Luck that they're not already famous. Or luck that the right person just happened to look up. In art as in love, one never knows how two people find each other, if they ever meet at all.

Just imagine how much courage it must take, to set a guitar case down on the cobblestones and make that first move, hoping it'll resonate with someone passing by. To keep pouring your heart into something, even if it falls on deaf ears. Reaching out in the face of indifference, just trying to give people permission to care.

Indifference is easy. It takes a lot of courage to fight back against it. So maybe we should stop and count ourselves lucky that there's still someone out there, fighting the good fight.

From *silent + brilliance*. In a 2007 experiment, violin virtuoso Joshua Bell tried his hand at busking in a subway station, playing for nearly an hour on his priceless Stradivarius. In the end, only seven of a thousand passersby stopped to listen. No applause. He collected $32. But as *Washington Post* writer Gene Weingarten observed, "Every single time a child walked past, he or she tried to stop and watch. And every single time, a parent scooted the kid away." Pronounced "*sil*-ee-uhns."

anti-aliasing

n. curiosity about the real flesh-and-blood people behind internet usernames, whose flamboyant uniqueness suggests that when our parents were searching our nameless faces looking for hints of who we would become, they really should have considered Mr. Cookieface, Unicornpuncher, Dutchess Von Whatever, or Wookiegasm.

In digital graphics, *anti-aliasing* is a technique to smooth the appearance of jagged pixels in low-resolution images.

kinchy

adj. feeling guilty that you care about your own petty concerns more deeply than faraway cataclysms—that a family spat hurts more than a civil war, that a three-day fever hits you harder than climate change.

Japanese 近視 (*kinshi*), near-sightedness. A word just shy of *kinship*. Pronounced "*kin*-chee."

mimeomia

n. the frustration of knowing how neatly you embody a certain stereotype, without even intending to; the sense of bafflement at the extent to which we all seem to hew to certain tropes, each looking pretty much how you'd expect them to look, as if we're all trick-or-treating through society wearing one of a handful of premade costumes, because we're tired of answering the question, "What are you supposed to be?"

Ancient Greek μῖμος (*mîmos*), imitator, actor + μῖσος (*mîsos*), hatred. Pronounced "mim-ee-*oh*-mee-uh."

scrough

v. intr. to mindlessly perform a tedious task that nobody will ever notice, required by a bureaucracy that nobody fully owns, in pursuit of outcomes that nobody really wants.

From *scrow*, to work hard + *scroff*, useless bits of leftover material + *cog*, a tiny forgettable element in a complicated machine. Pronounced "skrawg."

hemeisis

n. the off-putting awareness of how deeply your culture's norms are ingrained in your psyche—arbitrarily defining what you find shameful and admirable, private and communal, attractive and repulsive, fair and unfair—as if you'd been programmed in a way that you can't control or even perceive, until you happen to encounter someone who has slightly different code.

Ancient Greek ἡμεῖς (*hēmeîs*), we (excluding the listener). Pronounced "hem-*ey*-sis."

aftergloom

n. the pang of loneliness you feel the day after an intensely social event, as the glow of voices and laughter fades into a somber quiet.

From *afterglow* + *gloom*.

hobsmacked

adj. suddenly aware of how limited your social circles really are; that although your immediate environment feels like a microcosm of society, it's more like a bag of exotic fish floating on the surface of a huge aquarium, which is teeming with a million shadowy subcultures that you'd be stunned to see up close.

From *hobnob*, to mix socially + *gobsmacked*, astounded.

anthrodynia

n. a state of exhaustion with how cruel people can be, freely undercutting each other in ways that seem petty and gratuitous—which can sometimes trigger a countervailing sense of gratitude for things that are kind, sincere, forgiving, or unabashedly joyful.

Ancient Greek ἄνθρωπος (*ánthrōpos*), humanity + ὀδύνη (*odúnē*), sorrow, anguish, pain. Pronounced "an-thruh-*din*-ee-uh."

fygophobia

n. the fear that your connections with people will keep dwindling as you get older; that one by one, you'll all go flying off the merry-go-round in wildly different directions, sailing through various classes and jobs and interests, ultimately landing in far-flung neighborhoods where you'll hunker down with your families plus a handful of confidants you see a few times a year, perpetually reassuring each other, "We should keep in touch."

Greek φύγω (*fýgo*), I leave + -φοβία (*-phobía*), fear. Compare the Greek φυγόκεντρος (*fygókentros*), centrifuge. Pronounced "fahy-goh-*foh*-bee-uh."

Fig. 10. Ioche. | Collage by John Koenig | dictionaryofobscuresorrows.com

IOCHE

the anxiety of being an individual

Imagine how much courage it must take to come into this world all by yourself. It's almost like being tossed overboard. Nine months you spent in a state of symbiosis, lulled by the steady rhythm of the only home you've ever known—but then suddenly, at the moment of birth, you find yourself adrift in the open ocean, fighting to catch your breath, with nothing stable to hold on to. You're never very far away from another body, but now it's *another body*, that could come and go at any given moment. For the first time, the realization hits: you're on your own.

You never really get used to the feeling of being an individual. How strange it is that you're born alone and die alone. That you alone must carry your own body, and your own name. Nobody else can feel the pain you feel, or hear the ringing in your ears, or will ever be able to share an unforgettable dream. You alone manage this particular storehouse of memories, being the only one to remember certain things, or the only one to forget.

How strange it is that your life is the only one populated by this particular cast of characters. Strange to find yourself floating in a sea of swirling billions, only a few of whom you'll ever get a chance to know and trust. Which leaves you in a state of perpetual tension. You can follow the crowd for a while, but you'll never quite be able to relax, having to watch out in case they suddenly shift course or whip themselves up into groupthink. You're free to break out on your own, but you'll never feel all that free: as the sole protector and navigator, you'll find yourself perpetually looking over your shoulder, wondering if there's a good reason this particular road is the one less traveled. Strange that no matter how predictable your life is, nobody in history has ever lived it before. Strange to think that your concerns are your business and yours alone.

But strangest of all are those moments when you can almost transcend your singular nature, and feel yourself connecting with another human being. To be swept up by a choir, letting your bones melt into the vibration of a certain chord, thrumming in tune with a thousand other voices. To sit up with a friend all night talking freely and openly, never doubting that you're being heard, never having to wonder if you're being misunderstood. To fall into the swell of a shared ecstasy—coming achingly close to finding pleasure in another's pleasure.

Of course eventually the song ends and the sun rises, and we all carry on our own separate lives. And at the end of it, you may find yourself feeling all the more disconnected. Such is the curse of being an individual.

You may never get comfortable living life on your own. Maybe you'll never get over the initial shock of existing at all, and will spend your life as a perpetual newcomer, still trying to catch your breath, right until the last. But know that at the very least, you're in good company. Ask any one of us, and we'll tell you: *you're not alone.*

Italian *io che*, I who. Pronounced "*ahy*-uh-kee."

latigo

n. a dizzying sense of awe at the sheer scale of modern society—looking out at a city so vast and complex it can barely be mapped, with millions of miles of roads and power lines and water mains that must be continually repaired and replaced every few years, feeding a labyrinth of supply chains and regulations and contracts and algorithms—a system so massive that individual people seem almost beside the point, that if everybody were to vanish all at once, the city would sigh and carry on its business.

From *labyrinth*, a maze of tortuous complexity + *vertigo*, the whirling sensation of looking down from great heights. Compare Spanish *látigo*, whip. Pronounced "*lat*-i-goh."

innity

n. the complicated solitude of hotel rooms late at night, spending time in a place that's both yours and emphatically not yours, both soulless and homey, both timeless and temporary, suspended somewhere halfway between vacancy and no vacancy.

From *inn*, a small hotel or tavern for travelers + *inanity*, a total lack of meaning or ideas. Pronounced "*ihn*-i-tee."

wenbane

adj. feeling small and alone while walking the streets of an unfamiliar city, swept along in the commercial bustle of asphalt and neon, dwarfed by impenetrable monoliths looming high overhead, brushed aside by pulses of traffic carrying on their daily business, with nobody willing to look you in the eye except for the posters encrusted on subway walls, each of them pitching at someone other than you.

From *wen*, an enormously congested city that swells like a cyst + *bane*, an affliction or poison.

mal de coucou

n. a condition in which you have an active social life but very few close friends—people who you can trust, who you can be yourself with, who can help flush out the weird psychological toxins that tend to accumulate over time—which can eventually progress into a state of acute social malnutrition, where even if you devour an entire buffet of chitchat, you'll still feel pangs of hunger.

French *mal*, ache + *de coucou*, of the cuckoo bird. *Coucou* is also a French colloquialism for "Hey there!" *Mal de coucou* is a riff on the term *mal de caribou*, also known as *rabbit starvation*, in which you can starve to death even with unlimited access to lean meats like rabbit and caribou, after eating an excess of protein and not enough fat. Pronounced "mal duh koo-*koo*."

the unsharp mask

n. the tendency for social networks to magnify unexpected personality traits of people you know, a consequence of compressing someone's raw persona into a low-res digital format, which can randomly brighten their outer glow, sharpen their comic edges, darken their shadows, or add motion blur to a stationary life.

In digital photo processing, *unsharp mask* is a filter that combines the original negative with a blurred positive image. The resulting image may look sharper but is actually a less accurate interpretation of the subject.

heartmoor

n. the primal longing for a home village to return to, a place that no longer exists, if it ever did; the fantasy of finding your way back home before nightfall, hustling to bring in the cattle before the rains come; picturing a cluster of lanterns glowing on the edge of a tangled wood, hearing the rattle and hiss of meals cooking over a communal fire, finding your place in a crowded longhouse made of clay-packed thatch, where you'd sit and listen to the voices of four generations layered into a canon, telling stories of a time when people could still melt into a collective personality and weren't just floating around alone.

From *heart* + *moor*, to tie a boat to an anchor. Pronounced "*hahrt-moor.*"

LUTALICA

the sense that you're more than
the categories that society puts you in

You tell the world who you are in a million different ways. Some are subtle; some are not. A twang in your voice, a tattoo on your shoulder, a spring in your step, or a hole in your shoe. But somehow it doesn't seem to matter: this world has already got you pegged.

Soon after you were born, you were put in a little box with a label slapped on it. It was nothing personal—and that was kind of the point. It was an easy way to keep things organized, so people could size you up at a glance and didn't have to think about what was inside. Gradually you learned to make yourself comfortable, positioning yourself in relation to the expectations of others, subverting or reinforcing them as you will. You tried packaging and repackaging your identity in different combinations, until you began to feel like you belong, and could wear your labels proudly.

But there's a part of you that never found a home, rattling around in categories that never really did you justice. You look around at other people, trying to judge how loosely they fit in their own lives, sensing a knot of confusion hidden beneath a name tag. And you realize we're still only strangers, though we already think we know what the other is going to say. As if the only thing left to talk about is who belongs in what category, and which labels are right or wrong.

It's an open question why we sort ourselves into categories. Maybe it's the only way to stay sane in a society full of strangers, so you don't have to wade through a thicket of individuals just to pay for your groceries. We put people in boxes to get on with our day, to feel connected with each other, or feel like we're a part of something, because we're afraid that if there was nothing to contain us, we'd melt into the air.

You can't help but wonder what would happen if these boxes began falling apart. If each of us took the time to write our identities by hand, speaking only for ourselves, in our own words. Taking our chances out in the open, meeting each other as we are, in all our wholeness and strangeness. Finally gathering the courage to ask, "What is it like being you?"—while being brave enough to admit that we don't already know the answer.

Maybe it'll mean that we've finally arrived, unpacking the boxes to make ourselves at home. Maybe someday our grandchildren will listen to our stories of how we treated each other back in the day, and they'll struggle to believe it even happened in the first place. How could we manage to live in the same house for so long but never stop to introduce ourselves?

Serbo-Croatian *lútalica*, a wanderer or stray animal. Pronounced "loo-*tal*-i-kuh."

star-stuck

adj. exhausted by endless reviews and secondhand impressions; itching to stumble blindly into the world and make some mistakes, to wander around opening doors to restaurants and performances and movies you've never heard of, without the slightest idea of what to expect.

From *star*, a standard rating unit of reviews + *stuck*.

poggled

adj. shocked upon looking twice at something you see every day and catching an obvious detail you'd never noticed before—an old scar on your loved one's knee, a wall in your house that's apparently always been purple, or a prominent building that seemed to appear in your neighborhood overnight—which makes you wonder how much else of your world you might be missing, when you're just barely there yourself.

Macedonian поглед (*pogled*), a glimpse. Pronounced "*pog*-uhld."

gaudia civis

n. a humble pulse of gratification you feel when acting as a citizen—serving on a jury, standing in line at a polling place, taking part in a debate at a town meeting—where you can actually feel the gears of democracy turning ever so slightly, because you actually had a hand in it.

Latin *gaudia*, joys + *civis*, citizen. Pronounced "*gou*-dee-uh *siv*-is."

nyctous

adj. feeling quietly overjoyed to be the only one awake in the middle of the night—sitting alone with a laptop and a cup of tea or strolling down the center line of an abandoned street—taking in the world like an empty theater between productions, stripped down to a simple black box, open to be whatever you want it to be.

From *Nyctocereus*, a genus of cactus that blooms only at night. Pronounced "*nik*-tuhs."

FIVE

Boats Against the Current

HOLDING ON IN THE
RUSH OF THE MOMENT

The illimitable, silent, never-resting thing called Time, rolling, rushing on, swift, silent, like an all-embracing ocean-tide, on which we and all the Universe swim like exhalations, like apparitions which *are*, and then *are not*: this is forever very literally a miracle; a thing to strike us dumb—for we have no word to speak about it.

—THOMAS CARLYLE, *On Heroes*

Fig. 11. Zenosyne. | Collage by John Koenig | dictionaryofobscuresorrows.com

ZENOSYNE

the feeling that time is getting faster

It's actually just after you're born that your life flashes before your eyes. Entire eons are lived in those first few months. At first, time is only felt vicariously, as something that happens to other people. Looking out at the world from a car seat, you feel inseparable from the world itself, with nothing to do but watch it passing by. You get used to living in the moment, because there's nowhere else to go.

Before long, life begins to move, and you learn to move with it. You take it for granted that you're a different person every year, upgraded with a different body and a different future. You run around so fast, the world around you seems to stand still. A summer vacation can stretch on for an eternity.

We should consider the idea that youth is not actually wasted on the young. That their heightened emotions make perfect sense, once you adjust for inflation. For someone going through adolescence, life feels epic and tragic simply because it is—every kink in their day could easily warp the arc of their story.

Soon enough, the stakes of life begin to settle. You feel time moving forward, learning its rhythm, passing from one birthday to the next. Each time you circle back around, and cross the same point around the sun, and hear "Many happy returns." But you can already feel a shift in the pace of things, and get the feeling that each year is worth a little less than the last, as if your birthday arrives one day earlier every year.

As your twenties whirl into your thirties, you feel the circle begin to tighten, and all at once you realize it's a spiral, and you're already halfway through. You start to notice how much effort it takes just to hold on to what you have—catching up with friends, keeping up with your obligations, maintaining your possessions, clearing your head. As more of your day repeats itself, you keep trying to slow down and focus on the things that matter to you. You try to stay open to new experiences but find it harder and harder to resist the pull toward your center of gravity: the ballast of memories you hold on to, which occupy more and more of your attention.

Until you reach a point when it all seems to move under its own inertia. So even when you're holding still, settling down to bed at the end of a long day, it feels like you're running somewhere. And even if tomorrow you manage to run a little faster, and stretch your arms a little farther, you'll still feel the seconds slipping away as you drift around the bend.

Life is short—and life is long. But not in that order.

In philosophy, *Zeno's dichotomy paradox* asks how a person can walk from one point to another if they must first cross a seeming infinity of halfway points, which makes their journey look like a series of ever-shrinking steps + *Mnemosyne*, the personification of memory in Ancient Greek mythology. Pronounced "ze-*nos*-uhn-ee."

vellichor

n. the strange wistfulness of used bookstores, which are somehow infused with the passage of time—filled with thousands of old books you'll never have time to read, each of which is itself locked in its own era, bound and dated and papered over like an old room the author abandoned years ago, a hidden annex littered with thoughts left just as they were on the day they were captured.

From *vellum*, parchment + *ichor*, the fluid that flows in the veins of the gods in Ancient Greek mythology. Pronounced "*vel*-uh-kawr."

keir

n. an ill-fated attempt to reenact a beloved memory years later, returning to a place that once felt like home, only to find it now feels uncannily off, like walking through a wax museum of your own childhood.

Dutch *kier*, fissure or narrow opening, as in the midpoint of an hourglass. Pronounced "keer."

austice

n. a wistful omen of the first sign of autumn—a subtle coolness in the shadows, a rustling of dead leaves abandoned on the sidewalk, or a long skein of geese sweeping over your head like the second hand of a clock.

From *autumn* + *auspice*, an omen, or a divination derived from observing the actions of birds. Pronounced "*aw*-stis."

backmasking

n. the instinctive tendency to see someone as you knew them in their youth—a burned-in image of grass-stained knees, graffitied backpacks, or handfuls of birthday cake, superimposed on an adult with a mortgage, or children of their own.

In audio recording, *backmasking* is a technique wherein a sound is deliberately recorded backward, so it's only intelligible when played in reverse.

keta

n. a random image from your distant past that leaps back into your attention, that doesn't mean much of anything but is somehow able to keep fighting against the current, swimming back and forth in your mind, still developing.

After a species of salmon, *Oncorhynchus keta*, which "run" upstream to spawn every year, leaping back to the place they were born; they're not worth much commercially, but the ketas don't know that. When we look back on our lives, it's not just the moments that we remember, not the grand gestures and catered ceremonies, or the world we capture poised and smiling in photos. It's the little things—the minutes—the cheap raw material of ordinary time. Pronounced "*kay*-tuh."

aulasy

n. the sadness that there's no way to convey a powerful memory to people who weren't there at the time—driving past your childhood home to show it to a friend, or pointing at a picture of a loved one you lost, only to realize that to them it's just another house, just another face.

A contraction of *auld lang syne*, which is Scots for "times long past"—fragments of which are still present in *aulasy*, but the meaning has been lost. Pronounced "*awl*-uh-see."

enterhood

n. the set of living people who have known you all your life, all the way back to your infancy, before you had a clue who you were; a group that slowly shrinks as you get older, until the point when all of your closest confidants have only ever seen an abridged version of you, having joined your story somewhere in the middle of things, just as you did.

From *enter* + *entire* + *hood*.

keyframe

n. a moment that felt innocuous at the time but ended up marking a diversion into a strange new era of your life—a chance meeting you'd think back on for years, a harmless comment that sparked an ongoing feud, an idle musing that would come to define your entire career—a monumental shift secretly buried among the tiny imperceptible differences between one ordinary day and the next.

In video compression, a *key frame* defines major changes in a scene. Most frames in compressed video are *in-betweens*, marking subtle incremental changes, but key frames depict a whole new scene. This technique allows you to move forward without stopping to buffer, even if it makes it harder to rewind.

ANEMOIA

nostalgia for a time you never experienced

Looking at old photos, it's hard not to feel a kind of wanderlust. A pang of nostalgia, for an era you never lived through. Longing to step through the frame into a world of black and white, if only to sit on the side of the road and watch the locals passing by.

These are people who lived and died before any of us arrived here. Who sleep in some of the same houses we do, and look up at the same moon. Who breathe the same air, feel the same blood in their veins—and live in a completely different world.

It's a world still covered in dust from the frontier. A world of adults, whose lives are hammered out by hand. A world of front porches, of fires to light in the evening, of conversations over a fence. You'd feel the energy of the boulevards teeming with crowds, gathering to tell dirty jokes, awaiting news reports, or crisscrossing at random, just barely dodging the horses. You could hear the voices of hardscrabble homesteaders, calling in their children for their one and only family photo. Or look around at the architecture of the old city, whose ornate limestone canyons fade back into a ghostly haze, dotted here and there with people lounging in the windows, trying to escape the oppressive summer heat.

You'd watch as they carry on with their lives, that seem so important. Trying to read their faces, or look into their eyes, so piercing and otherworldly, their gaze fixed elsewhere. They have no way of knowing that their story has already been written. If only they could look around the way you could, they could relax and soak in the atmosphere of the moment.

Of course, to them, it wasn't all flickering silence and grainy black-and-white. They saw vivid color rushing by in three dimensions, heard voices in deafening stereo, confronted smells they couldn't escape. For them, nothing was ever simple. None of them knew for sure what this era meant, or that it was even an era to begin with. At the time, their world was real. Nothing was finished, and nothing was guaranteed.

That world is now gone. If the past is a foreign country, we're only tourists. We can't expect to understand the locals or why they do what they do. We can only ask them to hold still, so we can capture a photo to take home with us. So we can pretend to ourselves that we've learned anything at all about who they were, and what it was like to live in another time.

The photo itself means very little, in the end. Maybe all we ever wanted was the frame. So we could sit for a few minutes in a world of black-and-white, with clean borders that protect us from the rush of time. Like a tide pool just out of the reach of the waves—so clear and still, you can see your own reflection.

Ancient Greek ἄνεμος (*ánemos*), wind + νόος (*nóos*), mind. Compare *anemosis*, which occurs when a tree is warped by strong air currents until it seems to bend backward, leaning into the wind. Pronounced "an-uh-*moi*-uh."

thwit

n. a pang of shame when an embarrassing memory from adolescence rushes back into your head from out of nowhere, which is somehow no less painful even if nobody else remembers it happened in the first place.

Acronym of The Hell Was I Thinking?

appriesse

n. the feeling of loss that you never had a chance to meet a certain person before they died, which compels you to try to get to know them anyway, gathering snapshots and stories to build out a sketch of who they were, learning them like a character in a novel, which makes them feel all the more alive even though you've already skipped ahead and read the last page.

Latin *appretiare*, to appraise + *ad pressum*, after. Pronounced "ap-ree-*es*."

blinkback

n. the disillusionment of revisiting a pop-culture touchstone of your youth and finding that it hasn't aged well at all—having to confront its cringey dialogue, hand-puppet characterization, and wildly implausible plotting—which only makes you wonder what else in your mental fridge is past its expiration date.

Appalachian English (dialect) *blinked*, soured milk + *back*, in the past.

pithered

adj. frustrated that you can't force yourself to remember something, even though it's right on the tip of your tongue—wishing you could simply rifle through your own files directly, rather than having to toss random scraps to your team of mental archivists, who evidently need hours to sift through the pile before they come up with an answer, just as you're falling asleep.

From *pither*, to dig lightly. Pronounced "*pith*-erd."

fellchaser

n. a long-forgotten mistake from your past that could reappear at any time and rip your life apart, like a boomerang you tossed away years ago that's only just now looping back around, which you'd have no idea how to handle because you have no idea what it is.

From *fell*, to cause to fall by delivering a blow + *molechaser*, a low swooping throw of a boomerang.

yeorie

n. a certain scent that has the power to sweep you back to childhood—the acrid funk of bug spray, the earthy sweetness of dead leaves on wet asphalt, the rebellious twang of gasoline fumes in the summer heat.

From *yewthor*, a pungent scent + *yewre*, water-bearer. Pronounced "*yoh*-ree."

Fig. 12. Klexos. | Collage by Richard Vergez | Instagram @dickvergez

KLEXOS

the art of dwelling on the past

Your life is written in indelible ink. There's no going back to erase the past, tweak your mistakes, or fill in missed opportunities. When the moment's over, your fate is sealed. But if you look closer, the ink never really dries on any of your experiences. They can change their meaning the longer you look at them.

It's often said that there's nothing to be gained in looking backward. But there are ways of thinking about the past that aren't just nostalgia or regret; a kind of questioning that can allow fresh context to trickle in over the years, slowly filling out the picture like an inkblot painting, right there in front of you.

You can watch as a hero shrinks into someone deeply troubled, while a villain might begin to seem utterly relatable. A few peripheral characters might turn out to have been central to your story all along. A golden age can take on a darker edge, exposing cracks in a relationship you once thought was perfect. A wasted year can turn out to have been a shrewd investment, vital to your eventual success. The end of the world can be bargained down to a pivot point to something better. And a glancing wound from years ago might still be bleeding under the surface, having hurt you in ways that affect your entire life.

Time can even change your image of who you are. You may turn out to have been lucky when you thought you were cursed, cringeworthy when you thought you were cool, flawed when you thought you were quirky, cared for when you thought you were alone.

Maybe it's not so bad to dwell on the past, as long as it brings you closer to the truth. If nothing else, it's a way to push back against the oversimplification of time. Trying to keep a memory alive, as something more than just a caricature of itself.

Maybe we should think of memory itself as an art form, in which the real work begins as soon as the paint hits the canvas. And a work of art is never finished, only abandoned.

From *klecksography*, which is the art of making images from inkblots, famously used in Rorschach psychoanalytic tests. Interpreting their ambiguity is thought to illuminate the subconscious of the patient. Pronounced "*kleks*-ohs."

anchorage

n. the desire to hold on to time as it passes, like trying to keep your grip on a rock in the middle of a river, feeling the weight of the current against your chest while your elders float on downstream, calling over the roar of the rapids, *"Just let go—it's okay—let go."*

From *anchorage*, a port at which ships may anchor. Pronounced *"ang-ker-ij."*

daguerreologue

n. an imaginary conversation with an old photo of yourself, in which you might offer them a word of advice—to banish your worries, soak it all in, or shape up before it's too late—or maybe just ask them if they thought you had done justice to the life they built for you.

From *daguerreotype*, a form of early portrait photography + *dialogue*. Pronounced "duh-*gair*-uh-lawg."

kerisl

n. the sorrow of imagining the wealth of knowledge forever lost to history—knowing we'll never hear the language of the Etruscans, the battle cry of the Sea Peoples, or the burial chants of the Neanderthals; that we'll never read any more than a fragment of the works of Blake, Sappho, Aristotle, or Jesus; or enjoy the untold treasures of so many burned libraries and forgotten oral traditions and unrecorded songs—any of which might have made up the cornerstone of the canon, that we'd all be able to quote by heart and couldn't imagine living without.

A contraction of *Kergeulen Islands*. Roughly equidistant between Australia, Antarctica, and Madagascar, they are the only visible remnant of the Kergeulen microcontinent, which was submerged some twenty million years ago. Three times the size of Japan, it was once covered in dense conifer forests, with peaks reaching 2,000 meters above sea level, populated with strange and nameless fauna that must have called it home, before all traces were lost beneath the waves. Pronounced "*kair*-ahyl."

mithenness

n. the unsettling awareness that the rest of the world happily carries on in your absence, that although things only ever seem to change when you check back in for an update, they're unwilling to wait for you, and undergo massive shifts while your back is turned—your mother getting older, your old friends becoming different people, your hometown losing some of the hallmarks that made it feel like home.

Middle English *mithen*, to be hidden away. Pronounced "*mith*-uhn-nis."

MORII

the desire to capture a fleeting experience

Strange how strong the instinct is: to see something incredible and reach for a camera. As if you're trying to lend it some credibility. To prove that it's real. That *I was here.*

We live our lives in moments: in those rare experiences we stop to notice and carry with us, in the hopes of stringing them together, trying to tell a story. But even in the moment, you can already feel it start to fade. So you try to capture it and convert it into something that will last longer than just a flash.

A photo can feel more real than its subject. It lets you build a version of the world that you can take with you. A world flattened and simple. A world that doesn't change— that fits in the frame. A little brighter and more colorful, with everything under control.

You can travel the globe looking for memories and still find yourself standing behind a camera, waiting for the world to hold still. With every click of the shutter, you're trying to press Pause on your life. If only so you can feel a little more comfortable moving on, living in a world stuck on Play.

A part of you knows you can't take it with you. But that doesn't stop you from trying. It doesn't stop you from wondering, *What if I could stay just a little longer?* or *What if we didn't have to go?* We try to capture moments as if we're afraid they'll escape. But they'll get away eventually.

So go ahead: take one last look, one more shot—so that years from now you can flip back through and try to relive it all over again. But maybe even then, you'll be thinking to yourself, *Ah well. I guess you had to be there.*

From *memento mori*, a small reminder of your mortality + *torii*, traditional Japanese gates that mark the threshold between the profane and the sacred. Pronounced "*moh*-ree."

tirosy

n. a complicated feeling of envy and admiration for people younger than you—their eyes shining with energy, their futures rich with potential, their confidence smooth and untouched like a freshly opened jar of peanut butter, which you simultaneously want to preserve forever and gleefully undercut.

Latin *tiros*, beginners, new recruits + *jealousy*. Pronounced "*teer*-uh-see."

lap year

n. the age at which you become older than your parents were when you were born, which signals that your stage of the race has already begun, having spent years coasting in their slipstream as they tackled the mountain stages of life, leaving you strong, energetic, and deeply mortified by their loud yellow jerseys.

From *lap*, one full circuit around a course + *gap year*, a regenerative break between adjacent stages of life. In the Tour de France, the cyclist with the lowest time receives a ceremonial yellow jersey and the right to start the next stage.

etterath

n. the feeling of emptiness after a long and arduous process is finally complete—having finished school, recovered from surgery, or gone home at the end of your wedding—which leaves you relieved that it's over but missing the stress that organized your life into a mission.

Norwegian *etter*, after + *råtne*, decay. Pronounced "*et*-er-rath."

Fig. 12. Avenoir. | Collage by Marcos Guinoza | Instagram @marcosguinoza | *Boat Cloud* | 2020

AVENOIR

the desire to see your memories in advance

We take it for granted that life moves forward. You build memories, you build momentum. But you move as a rower moves: facing backward. You can see where you've been, but not where you're going. And your boat is steered by a younger version of you. It's hard not to wonder what life would be like facing the other way.

If your life ran backward, everything would have a sense of order, settling over time into a beautiful simplicity. You'd see your memories approaching for years and watch as they slowly became real. You'd know in advance which friendships will last, which days will prove important, and you could prepare in advance for upcoming mistakes. You wouldn't have to wonder how much time you had left with people, or how their lives would turn out. You'd know from the start which week was the happiest you'll ever be, so you could cherish every second of it, soaking it in while it lasts.

Your life would expand into epic drama. The colors would get sharper, the world would feel bigger. One by one, you'd patch things up with old friends, enjoying one last conversation before you meet and go your separate ways. Your family would drift slowly together, finding each other again. You'd fall out of old habits until you could picture yourself becoming almost anything. You'd graduate backward through school, and gradually learn to forget, first the little things, then the big things, gradually stripping away everything you didn't need to know. You'd become nothing other than yourself, reveling in your own weirdness.

And then the world would finally earn your trust, until you'd think nothing of jumping freely into things, into the arms of other people. You'd remember what home feels like, and decide to move there for good. You'd grow smaller as the years pass, as if trying to give away everything you had before leaving. You'd try everything one last time, until it all felt new again. Then you'd start to notice that each summer feels longer than the last, until you reach the long coasting retirement of childhood.

You'd become generous and give everything back. Pretty soon you'd run out of things to give, things to say, things to see. By then you'll have found someone perfect, and they'll become your world. And you will have left this world just as you found it. Nothing left to remember, nothing left to regret, with your whole life laid out in front of you, and your whole life left behind.

French *avenir*, future + *avoir*, to have. Pronounced "av-uh-*nwar*."

echthesia

n. a state of confusion when your own internal sense of time doesn't seem to match that of the calendar—knowing that something *just happened* though it apparently took place seven years ago, or that you somehow built up a decade of memories in the span of only a year and a half.

Greek εχθές (*echthés*), yesterday + αἴσθησις (*aísthēsis*), sensation. Pronounced "ek-*thee*-zhuh."

walloway

n. a sense memory you've mulled over so thoroughly that it's become totally drained of emotion—having replayed an old song to death, over-binged a favorite sitcom, or spent too much time in the old neighborhood—inadvertently depleting a wellspring of nostalgia by watering it down with newer connotations.

From *wallow*, to indulge or soak in something + *away*. Pronounced "*wol*-uh-wey."

nowlings

n. the total set of human beings alive at any given time, a group that nudges slightly forward whenever a new baby is born or the world's oldest person dies, and turns over completely every hundred years or so; a random assemblage of billions of contemporaries who you feel an odd sense of connection to, because whatever problems we might face right now, we're all facing them simultaneously.

From *now*, the present moment + *-lings*, inhabitants of.

emorries

n. vivid memories of a certain experience that you carry in your head for years until they're casually disputed by someone who remembers it very differently—correcting basic chronology, clarifying a misread gesture, or adding context you never knew—which makes you want to look again at all the images you've been using to piece together your worldview, wondering what details might've been hidden in shadow all this time, or washed out by your own naïveté.

After documentary filmmaker Errol Morris, whose work often addresses the fallibility of memory and how little of reality can be captured in a photograph. Pronounced "*em*-uh-reez," like *memories*, but with a piece missing.

KENOPSIA

the eeriness of places left behind

You can sense it when you move out of a house—noticing just how empty a place can feel. Walking through a school hallway in the evening, an unlit office on a weekend, or fairgrounds out of season. They're usually bustling with life but now lie abandoned and quiet.

It's easy to forget that most of your memories happened in places that are still around, the walls mostly unchanged, carrying on in your absence. But the world you once knew, and the people you still remember, have long since moved on, replaced by so many others who have passed through these doors.

It's almost impossible to imagine while you're still in it, knowing abstractly that the crowds will soon be gone, the lights shut off, the music silenced. If you spend enough time in a place, it becomes infused with a certain meaning, with specific memories soaked deep into every corner of the room. It's hard to imagine that it could ever mean anything else.

But soon enough, there will come a day when you'll pack up your things and walk through your house one last time. Looking slowly around the rooms, thinking back on everything that happened here. Which makes it feel not just empty but hyper-empty, with a total population in the negative, whose inhabitants are so conspicuously absent they glow like neon signs.

And not a day after you leave, it'll become someone else's new home. A blank canvas they'll fill up with their own memories, burying the life you built in a fresh coat of paint, leaving nothing but echoes of what was once here.

Maybe that's why we want to believe in ghosts. Maybe it's just a fantasy. A fantasy that our memories are so powerful that they'll leave a mark on the wall that would mean something to someone else and can't just be painted over. We just want to mark our time here, to keep the rooms filled and the memories alive.

If our houses ever feel haunted, it'll be because we're haunting them ourselves, trying to revisit all the places we once knew. As if there were something still there for us, something we forgot. As if there were ever such a thing as "unfinished business."

Ancient Greek κενό (*kenó*), emptiness + -οψία (*-opsía*), seeing. Pronounced "ken-*op*-see-uh."

alpha exposure

n. the otherworldly aura of seeing recordings of a friend in early childhood—catching those little gestures you'd one day come to know, so recognizable yet so foreign, searching their eyes for traces of who it is they'd eventually become.

From *alpha*, the unstable initial release of software still being tested + *exposure*, the amount of time that light is allowed onto photographic film.

clockwise

adj. aware that you'll only ever be a certain age relative to your loved ones, only seeing them from one arbitrary angle across the decades—never knowing your mother in her rebellious youth, never seeing your grandkid as anything other than a kid—because even though your life spans do happen to overlap, they'll never quite line up.

From *clock* + *wise*, pointedly aware of.

rasque

n. a moment you instantly wish you could take back, feeling a pulse of dread right after crossing the point of no return—a blurted confession, a hurled insult, a final decision you'd been waffling over for months—wanting to take just one step backward in time, reverting to the way things used to be, in the halcyon days of just a minute ago.

From *rue*, to regret + *bourrasque*, a tempest. Pronounced "rask."

anticious

adj. wondering what our ancestors would think of all this; haunted by the awareness that our world was designed by the dead, who spent their lives trying to flesh out every detail but never got to see how it all turned out—who might well think of the present as an impossible dream, a missed opportunity, or the end of the world as they knew it.

From *antecedent*, predecessor or ancestor + *anxious*. Pronounced "an-*tish*-uhs."

cullaways

n. the scattering of memories that your brain is actively forgetting at any given moment, erasing them one by one with no input from you and no knowledge that it's happening at all—which means that when you wake up in the morning, your past will feel imperceptibly altered, with no trace of what you ate last week, a party you attended ten years ago, or the first real conversation you had with your grandfather.

From *cull*, to control the size of a herd by selectively killing some animals + *away*. Pronounced "*kuhl*-uh-weys."

midsummer

n. the point in your mid-twenties when your youthfulness expires as a valid excuse, leaving you accountable for your own station in life, even if you're still only reeling from your past or planning for the future—which somehow makes time itself feel more urgent than before, until even the springtime pollen floating in the air reminds you of the coming snow.

Borrowed from the traditional feast of the summer solstice, after which all the days become shorter.

halfwise

adj. suddenly aware that you're more than halfway through a vacation or semester or other positive experience, noticeably closer to the end than the beginning, as if someone had flipped your mental hourglass overnight, turning a rush of fun surprises into a trickle of last hurrahs.

Norwegian Bokmål *halvveis*, halfway.

Fig. 13. Tichloch. | Collage by Errin Ironside | errinironside.com

TICHLOCH

the anxiety of never knowing
how much time you have left

Time is an odd sort of currency. You're free to spend it or squander it as you will, but no matter how you choose to budget your remaining years, they're only ever dispensed in tiny micropayments, cent by cent, heartbeat by heartbeat, tick after tock after tick.

Which means you have no way of knowing how much of it you have left. Maybe you're just now coming down to your last dime. Or maybe you're sitting on a vast fortune, with many decades still to come—but even then, you'd have no way of knowing it until it's too late, when you finally look around and conclude you must've been rich all along.

But suppose it was possible to check your remaining balance, knowing exactly how many heartbeats you had left in your lifetime. Most human beings will top out at around two billion beats, more with good behavior. Would it feel humbling to see your life distilled into a string of digits, gently ticking down? Or would it feel oddly comforting? After all, if you knew your time was short, you'd have no reason not to live each day as if it was your last, knowing how close that was to being true. And if your number was still in the billions, you could bank on a long retirement, kicking back and taking a little time for yourself, feeling like a billionaire.

At first. But then, in quiet moments, you'd start to notice a certain rhythm throbbing in your ears, like a clock you'd managed to tune out for months, only to hear it punctuate the silence with a *tick, tick, tick*. Whenever you settled down to sleep, you'd find it hard to ignore the feeling of your heart heaving around in its cage, pounding out its rhythm, which only seems to get faster the more you think about it. With every beat, you'd feel your fortune being withdrawn, cent by cent, a steady deposit of coins rattling down into a deep metal tray.

How long would it be before you'd start hoarding time, turning over every moment in your mind, looking for a price tag? You'd become all too aware how much life you keep trading for a pittance of salary, aware that tying your shoelaces wrong will cost you twenty beats, that posting a comment online might set you back three hundred, all of which might've been better spent elsewhere. You'd come to the end of a bad movie and whisper to yourself with some urgency, "That's two hours of my life I'm never getting back."

Alas. You're never getting any of it back. It's the cost of doing business. And even if you could have it appraised down to the fraction of a second, its value would be no clearer. Time has no inherent value. If it's a currency, it's a kind of fiat currency, in that you can't just cash it in for anything solid. Which means it's up to you to decide what it's worth trading for.

It may be a blessing that you never know how much time you have left, because it leaves you no other option but to listen to your heart and get into its rhythm, so you can focus on the things that make life worth living. So go ahead: make every second count, or don't. Seize the day or while away the hours. All you have is this moment. That alone is a blessing. You're almost out of time, and you have all the time in the world.

Acronym of The Insatiable Crocodile Hunts (What's) Left of Captain Hook. Pronounced "*tik*-lok."

ecury

n. a conversation that spans huge intervals of time, kept alive by contributors who casually overlay their thoughts as if no time had passed, which effectively compresses it all into a poignant temporal mash—an online thread that waits years between replies, a constitution being amended by successive generations, or a cave painting fleshed out in sessions ten thousand years apart, by artists who might each have been using the same discarded piece of charcoal.

Basque *ekurrikatz*, a piece of charcoal used for drawing. Pronounced "*ek*-yuh-ree."

archimony

n. anger about an injustice you only discovered long after the fact, after years have passed and everyone else has moved on, leaving you seething with an awkward and antiquated righteousness that you're not sure what to do with, like a flywheel still spinning long after the engine is shut off.

From *archi-*, earlier, primitive + *acrimony*, bitterness, animosity. Pronounced "*ahr*-kuh-moh-nee."

zysia

n. the sense that you were born too early in history, all too aware of how crude and backward the present can be, feeling tired of having to sit through so much clunky exposition and slow-burning suspense, when all you want to do is skip ahead to find out what happens next.

A word tantalizingly close to being the last word of the dictionary, but not quite there. Pronounced "*zee*-zhah."

aftersome

adj. astonished to think back on the bizarre sequence of accidents that brought you to where you are today—as if you'd spent years bouncing down a Plinko pegboard, passing through a million harmless decision points, any one of which might've changed everything—which makes your long and winding path feel fated from the start, yet so unlikely as to be virtually impossible.

Swedish *eftersom*, because.

heart of aces

n. the awareness that although a certain experience may strike you as utterly unremarkable, it might be having a profound effect on other people nearby, who will remember every detail for the rest of their lives—having inspired the birth of a phobia, a fetish, a lifelong relationship, or a lifelong career.

In poker and blackjack, the ace card can be valued either low or high; it's up to the player to decide. Every day is an ace, which might end up being valuable or worthless, forgettable or unforgettable, depending on who's playing and what else they're holding in their hand.

o'erpine

v. intr. to wander through the grounds of a cemetery, glancing over the gravestones as if you were people-watching the dead, imagining all the things they must have seen and the lives they might have led, trying to conjure up an entire biography from a handful of words and dates etched in granite, with barely more than a single dash to cover the unimaginable vastness of their experience.

From *over*, finished and done with + *pine*, to yearn or grieve for something. Compare the flowering perennial *orpine*, also called *autumn joy* or *live-forevers*, which is often found in open sunny areas of cemeteries. Pronounced "*awr*-pahyn."

DÈS VU

*the awareness that this moment
will become a memory*

You were born on a moving train. Even though it feels like you're holding still, time is sweeping past you, right where you sit. But once in a while you look up, and start to feel the inertia, sensing the present moment already turning into a memory, even as it's still happening. Somehow you know in advance that you're going to remember this day for years to come.

You can almost feel the presence of your future self, looking back on this moment. Of course, by then it'll mean something very different. Maybe you'll cringe and laugh, or brim with pride, aching to return. Or you'll focus in on some random detail hidden in the scene—a future landmark making its first appearance, or discreetly taking its final bow.

So you look around the scene, trying to tell in advance what this moment is going to mean. It's as if you're walking through the memory while it's still happening, feeling for all the world like a time traveler.

You notice how strange it all seems. All the quaint little gadgets and fads and slang terms that never made all that much sense. All the faces around you, still so young and vibrant, fretting about the day's concerns, not yet realizing that this world is already out of their hands. That all of this will soon be swept away and replaced by something different. And yet nobody is stopping to take it all in or revel in the nostalgia of a world that once was. For them, and for you, it's still a bit too early for that.

In a way, you really are a time traveler, leaping into the future in little, tentative steps. A part of you is like a kid stuck in a strange land without a map, with nothing to do but soak in the moment and take one last look before moving on. But another part of you is already an old man looking back on things, waiting at the door for his granddaughter, who's trying to make her way home for a visit.

You are two people, separated by an ocean of time. Part of you bursting to talk about what you saw. Part of you longing to tell you what it all means.

French *dès vu*, seen as of now. Alternately *sera vu*, will be seen. Akin to the feeling of *déjà vu*, but in the reverse order—already remembering something as you're living it. Pronounced "dey *voo*."

spinning playback head

n. the disorienting feeling of meeting back up with an old friend and realizing that you've become different people on divergent paths—that even though they're standing right in front of you, the person you once knew isn't really there anymore.

After the part of a VCR that reads the signal on a videotape.

inerrata

n. a kind of mistake you wouldn't take back even if you could; the reluctance to disown a broken relationship or agonizing experience that has since become part of who you are, and trying to disown it would mean you're trying to live some other life.

Latin *in-*, not + *errata*, mistakes in a printed work. Pronounced "in-eh-*rah*-tuh."

present-tense

adj. intimidated by the awareness that you're in the present moment, right now, inhabiting the single fleeting second that exists, feeling like a surfer riding a cresting wave across an infinite sea, desperate to keep your balance, but unsure whether to lean forward or lean back.

From *present*, the moment at hand + *tense*, in a state of nervous strain.

affogatia

n. the weird loneliness of antiquated fads and memes and one-hit wonders, which tried so hard to capture their own era that they inadvertently became embedded in it.

Italian *affogato*, drowned. Pronounced "ah-fuh-*gat*-yuh."

epistrix

n. a disconcerting cluster of endings that all seem to happen at once; a random barrage of departures and closures and divorces and series finales and celebrity deaths, which leaves you anxiously aware that the author of your story seems to be wrapping up an awful lot of loose ends.

Ancient Greek ἐπὶ- (*epi-*), on top of + ὕστριξ (*hystrix*), a porcupine. To sit on a porcupine is to feel the pain of too many endings all at once. Pronounced "ih-*pis*-triks."

solla, solla, solla

n. an incantation whispered privately to yourself to celebrate the loss of something or someone you loved, which almost makes it feel like a deliberate renunciation, consciously deciding to relinquish them to an earlier part of your life.

Latin *solla*, whole, unbroken + Sesotho *fasolla*, to disconnect + Estonian *las olla*, let it be. Pronounced "suh-*lah*, suh-*lah*, suh-*lah*."

Fig. 14. Olēka. | Collage by Carolina Chocron | Instagram @carolina_chocron

OLĒKA

the awareness of how few days are memorable

Your life is a highlight reel. You'd like to think that every moment has potential, that there's something transcendent hidden all around. If you'd only stop to seize the day, you could hold on to it and carry it with you. But the truth is, most of life is forgotten instantly, almost as it's happening. Chances are that even a day like today will slip through your fingers and dissolve into oblivion, washed clean by the tides.

Another day, another week, another year: such is the rhythm of ordinary time. Filled with long, featureless stretches we tend to skip over to get to the good parts. The thousand acts of maintenance you have to do every day. The labor of keeping your body going, hauling it back and forth across the same stretch of road, no closer than you were the day before. You keep breathing in and out. Things fall apart; you clean up the mess. And it all washes away in the night, to be built up again in the morning. You keep throwing the week against the wall to see what sticks, hoping you'll remember something that happened today. Anything.

You begin to question how you're spending your life, wondering if you're wasting it. Spending so much energy just pushing back against the current, trying to keep your small boat afloat. Waiting for those singular moments that'll make it all worthwhile, when you can finally say, "*Eureka! I've found it!*"

But the rest of life is happening anyway, whether you'll remember it or not. So you might as well say, "*Olēka! I've lost it!*" As if to mark the passage of yet another morsel of life, flushed down the hourglass. A final toast to the endless forgotten days, whose humble labor has given you everything you have, at least for the moment.

As the song says: "Long live the high tide and long live the low, but above all, long live the difference."

Greek ἀπολώλεκα (*apolóleka*), I've lost it. The lyric quoted at the end is from Nada Surf's song "Là Pour Ça." In the original French: "Vive la marée haute et vive la basse, / Mais surtout vive la différence." Pronounced "oh-*lee*-kuh."

lisolia

n. the satisfaction of things worn down by time—broken-in baseball mitts, the shiny snout of a lucky bronze pig, or footprints ground deep into floorboards by generations of kneeling monks.

Italian *liso*, worn down, threadbare + *oliato*, oiled. Pronounced "lih-*soh*-lee-uh."

harke

n. a painful memory that you look back upon with un-expected fondness, even though you remember having dreaded it at the time; a tough experience that has since been overridden by the pride of having endured it, the camaraderie of those you shared it with, or the satisfaction of having a good story to tell.

From *hark back*, a command spoken to hunting dogs to retrace their course so they can pick up a lost scent. Pronounced "hahrk."

amentalio

n. the sadness of realizing that you're already forgetting sense memories of the departed—already struggling to hear their voice, picture the exact shade of their eyes, or call to mind the quirky little gestures you once knew by heart.

Greek αμήν (*amēn*), amen + μενταλιό (*mentalió*), locket. Pronounced "ah-men-*tal*-yoh."

énouement

n. the bittersweetness of having arrived here in the future, finally learning the answers to how things turned out but being unable to tell your past self.

French *énouer*, to pluck defective bits from a stretch of cloth + *dénouement*, the final part of a story, in which all the threads of the plot are drawn together and everything is explained. Pronounced "ey-noo-*mahn*."

YU YI

the longing to feel things intensely again

The first note is always the loudest. The conductor snaps their baton, the strings slash their bows, and the symphony thunders to life before settling down into a reverberating hum.

So it is with every new experience. How quickly each feeling starts to fade as you recalibrate your expectations. Maybe that's why your childhood could feel so intense, because you were steadily burning your way through a roster of firsts. The more you repeat an experience, the less you feel its impact, almost as if your brain is gradually tuning out the world.

But sometimes you reach a point when you can't feel anything at all, just a ringing in your ears—until like Beethoven, you find yourself pounding the keys of your life, trying to make the ground thunder below your feet. It makes you wish you could look around with fresh eyes, and feel things just as powerfully as you did when you felt them for the first time.

When you were a kid, you could still get *excited* about things. You felt that pirate's itch on the last day of school, the morning of your birthday, or the final turn toward your grandparents' house. You could feel rich from the coins in your pocket or being offered a piece of gum. You remember how big the world used to be, how wandering into the next neighborhood felt like stepping into a foreign country.

Adults swept over you like giants. Every rule was a decree, every sentence a life sentence.

Time moved differently then, if it moved at all, arriving in big scholastic chunks, and each arrival felt *major*. You'd start up the school year like a witness protection program, ready to be assigned new teachers, new skills, a new identity. In the summer, you could make an afternoon last all week long, riding bikes with friends or watching a trickle of water feel its way through the dirt. There were no phones buzzing in your pockets, no schedules, no hormones, no distractions— or maybe it was all distractions. Whatever it was, you tried to keep it going as long as you could, even after the streetlights turned on in the evening and you heard voices in the dark, already calling you home.

The kaleidoscope of your emotions spun wildly through-out the day, all of it intense. You could walk along howling or weeping or grinning like a goon. When you loved someone, you loved them openly and with abandon, squeezing hugs as hard as you could. When you found something funny, you could laugh so hard your diaphragm ached, your cheeks wet with tears, your temples throbbing. You could plunge into a book and come out gasping, stumble out of a movie looking at faces and colors differently, listen to a song on loop for weeks and feel it grab you by the throat every time. And you knew how to *play*, knew how to make your toys come alive in front of you, how to listen for their weird little voices.

But somehow, even then, a part of you understood that

this intensity wasn't going to last. There were moments late in childhood when you tried going back to play with your old favorite toys again, almost as a guilty pleasure, only to find you couldn't do it anymore. They looked just the same, as you turned them over in your hands—but suddenly they felt like bits of fabric and molded plastic, with nothing left to say.

You'll never feel same sense of peace you once felt, drifting off to sleep in the back seat of a car, only to find yourself teleported back into your own bed. You'll never have friendships that occupy so much of your attention, spending hours together every day for months, which made even the slightest betrayal sting. You'll never feel the mortifying terror of a middle-school bully or the heartrending agony of an unrequited crush. You should only hope that life never punches you in the gut the way it did then.

Still, every once in a while you catch yourself humming along to some silly pop song that once broke your heart at sixteen, trying to tap back into that feeling again. That was once your entire life. It was only a matter of time before the world took notice and turned down the volume.

The music is still in there somewhere, even if you can't hear the notes. Besides, there's some beauty left in echoes—in knowing you have a part to play and playing it well, in concert with those around you. And there are those rare moments when you can let yourself go, close your eyes and let your body move with the orchestra, the way that old trees swing back and forth in a windstorm.

You have to wonder what you're missing, closing your eyes like that. No matter; keep playing. Play as well as you can, and let some other soul get swept away for a moment or two. Until like Beethoven, you look up from the keys and ask yourself, *"Ist es nicht schön?"*

"Is it not beautiful?"

Ancient Chinese 余忆 (*yú yì*), I remember. Compare the Mandarin 玉衣 (*yù yī*), jade suit. Before their burial, the corpses of Han dynasty royals were clothed in ceremonial garments made of jade—a stone believed to have preservative properties. Even then, thousands of years ago, people were trying to protect themselves from the ravages of time by becoming "jaded." Pronounced "yoo yee."

SIX

Roll the Bones

CONNECTING THE DOTS
OF A WIDE-OPEN UNIVERSE

We can never know what to want, because, living only one life, we can neither compare it with our previous lives nor perfect it in our lives to come. [. . .] We live everything as it comes, without warning, like an actor going on cold. And what can life be worth if the first rehearsal for life is life itself? That is why life is always like a sketch. No, "sketch" is not quite the word, because a sketch is an outline of something, the groundwork for a picture, whereas the sketch that is our life is a sketch for nothing, an outline with no picture.

—MILAN KUNDERA, *The Unbearable Lightness of Being*

What, what am I to do with all of this life?

—GWENDOLYN BROOKS, *Maud Martha*

galagog

n. the state of being simultaneously entranced and unsettled by the vastness of the cosmos, which makes your deepest concerns feel laughably quaint, yet vanishingly rare.

From *galaxy*, a gravitationally bound system of millions of stars + *agog*, awestruck. Pronounced "*gal*-uh-gawg."

ellipsism

n. the sadness that you'll never be able to know how history will turn out, that you'll dutifully pass on the joke of being alive without ever learning the punch line, which may not suit your sense of humor anyway and will probably involve how many people it takes to change a lightbulb.

From *ellipsis*, a marker of a continuation that you don't get to see. Pronounced "ih-*lip*-siz-uhm."

boorance

n. an unassuming feature of our daily lives that will eventually come off as the bizarre relic of a bygone era, that'll make us look back in shock that we ever thought it was normal to bless each other's sneezes, drive cars by hand, swim in chlorinated pools, keep animals in zoos, or feel clean using little else but toilet paper—things that we never think to question, because that's just what people did "back then."

From *boor*, an ill-mannered person + *hence*, in the future from now. Pronounced "*boor*-uhns."

suerza

n. a feeling of quiet amazement that you exist at all; a sense of gratitude that you were even born in the first place, that you somehow emerged alive and breathing despite all odds, having won an unbroken streak of reproductive lotteries that stretches all the way back to the beginning of life itself.

Spanish *suerte*, luck + *fuerza*, force. Pronounced "soo-*wair*-zuh."

future-tense

adj. sensing the judgment of your future self looking over your shoulder—chuckling at your well-laid plans or clutching their pearls at the risky move you're about to make—which leaves you faintly wary of their opinion, even though you know they'd take your place in a heart-beat.

From *future* (the grammatical tense) + *tense*.

elosy

n. the fear of major life changes, even ones you've been anticipating for years; the dread of leaving behind the bright and ordinary world you know, stepping out into that liminal space before the next stage of life begins, like the dark and rattling void between adjoining metro cars.

Malagasy *lelosy*, snail, which is a creature that carries many twists and turns wherever it goes, trying in vain to outrun them. Pronounced "*ehl-uh-see*."

hem-jawed

adj. feeling trapped inside your own language, struggling to shake away the baggage weighing down certain words, unable to break out of its age-old structures and melodies, frustrated that the scattering of verbal pigments on its palette could never quite capture the colors in your head.

From *hem*, an attempt to clear the throat + *jaw*, coarse babble.

NODUS TOLLENS

*the sense that your life
doesn't fit into a story*

Your life is a story. A torrent of overlapping moments, rushing at you in no particular order. As the days flip past, it all happens far too quickly to absorb—a mess of seemingly random events. Every once in a while, you look back and highlight certain memories as important, as turning points in the main plot. You trace each thread back to its origin, finding omens and ironies scattered along the way, until it all feels inevitable, and your life makes sense.

But there are times when you look up and realize that the plot of your life doesn't make sense to you anymore. You thought you were following the arc of the story, but you keep finding yourself immersed in passages you don't understand. Either everything seems important or nothing does. It's just a tangled mess of moments that keeps changing depending on what you choose to highlight.

You look around and wonder, *What kind of story is this?* Just another coming-of-age tale, the same one your parents told, with the names switched around? Is your everyday life part of the origin story of something truly epic? Are you unwittingly getting by on other people's charity, mistaking your own luck for your own success? Are you a character in a romance, a tragedy, a travelogue, or just another cautionary tale?

As you thumb through the years, you may never know where this all is going. The only thing you know is that there's more to the story. That soon enough you'll flip back to this day looking for clues of what was to come, rereading all the chapters you tried to skim through to get to the good parts— only to learn that all along, you were supposed to choose your own adventure.

Latin *nodus tollens*, literally "the knot that denies by denying." In propositional logic, *modus tollens* (with an *m*) is a kind of argument that goes like this: "If P, then Q. But Q is not. Therefore, P must not be." Also known as going back and questioning your first assumptions when things don't work out the way you expected. Pronounced "*noh*-dus *tah*-luhns."

rookish

adj. feeling a vague longing for some sort of monarch to look down upon us from a high and distant castle, which you'd imagine would pacify the squabbling chaos of civic life and drastically narrow the range of choices and issues you have to think about, finally freeing you up from bearing the microscopic fraction of a crown that forever hangs over your head.

From the chess move of castling, which is when a rook rushes to protect the king, nearly swapping places with him.

kadot

n. fear of the prospect of not existing one day, feeling like a student about to graduate from the universe, on the cusp of a transition you don't feel ready for.

Finnish *kadotus*, perdition, which once meant "loss" but now means "eternal damnation." Pronounced "kuh-*doh*."

aoyaoia

n. a musical flavor found in electric guitar solos that compels you to snarl, squint, and arch your spine like a yowling jungle cat.

Onomatopoeic to the wail of an electric guitar. Pronounced "ow-*yow*-yuh."

dystoria

n. a feeling of irrelevance from the broader forces of history; the sense that your life has no relationship to any great mission, no generational hardship, not even an enemy—feeling as harmless as a droplet skittering down a window, that could've just as easily taken part in a tidal wave.

Latin *dys-*, bad + *historia*, history. Pronounced "dis-*toh*-ree-uh."

craxis

n. the unease of knowing how quickly your circumstances could change on you—that no matter how carefully you shape your life into what you want it to be, the whole thing could be overturned in an instant, with little more than a single word, a single step, a phone call out of the blue, and by the end of next week you might already be looking back on this morning as if it were a million years ago, a poignant last hurrah of normal life.

Latin *crāstinō diē*, tomorrow + *praxis*, the process of turning theory into reality. Pronounced "*krak*-sis."

aimonomia

n. the fear that learning the name of something—a bird, a constellation, an attractive stranger—will somehow ruin it, inadvertently transforming a lucky discovery into a conceptual husk pinned in a glass case, leaving one less mystery fluttering around in the universe.

French *aimer*, to love + *nom*, name. A palindrome. Pronounced "eym-uh-*nohm*-ee-uh."

Fig. 15. Witherwill. | Collage by John Koenig | dictionaryofobscuresorrows.com

WITHERWILL

the longing to be free of responsibility

Surely nothing is more empowering than knowing that you're free to do as you please. And yet there's something vaguely unsettling about it. There's a heaviness to the thought, when by all rights it should feel lofty and liberating. Because if it's true that you're in control of your own destiny, it must also be true that *you alone are in control*. That whatever fate ends up befalling you, it'll have your name written all over it. Which leaves you cursed with a feeling of perpetual responsibility, left with nobody to blame but yourself.

Of course, none of us is ever fully in control of our lives. Everyone you meet is fighting some sort of battle. You can only wonder how many of your decisions were secretly preordained or precluded by forces outside your control—by history or prejudice, biology or dumb luck. At the end of most days, you can fairly shrug off the weight of your daily misfortunes, reassuring yourself, *It wasn't your fault.* But soon enough you'll start to wonder, *Okay . . . now what?* And you'll start to feel the burden of tomorrow land on your shoulders.

Such is the blessing and the curse of being an adult. Life is certainly richer than it was when you were a kid, and it's a tremendous feeling to know that you're beholden to no one. But life is not nearly as fun as it once was, in part because now you're on the hook for it. By this point you know all too well that you'll have to pay for whatever silly little things you do, even though the cost is rarely clear ahead of time. It's like shopping in a store without price tags. You think you have a pretty good idea what things cost, but then you start to wonder if you might've been guessing wrong, unwittingly building up a debt you'll have to pay back for years. Somehow that doesn't matter; you're going to have to deal with it anyway. What else can you do but make your choices, make your bets, and make your peace with not knowing what happens next.

Still, there's a part of you that longs to be free to do as you please, without having to carry the burden of freedom. As you make your way through the day, your brain is hard at work trying to come up with excuses, trying to argue away your ownership of your own life. That's why you feel mysteriously drawn toward certain situations that just happen to let you off the hook. Perhaps you lean on deadlines to force your hand at the last minute, or put everyone else's desires before your own. You might be tempted to define yourself by victimhood or self-diagnosis, as if all of your flaws were merely symptoms of some huge systemic problem outside your control. Maybe you lose yourself in work or play or drunkenness, or surrender to the arbitrary dictates of your own moods. Perhaps you have a habit of dreaming of epic tales and cosmic forces, as if worldly concerns don't really matter. Or you simply try to do as little as possible, thinking it's safer than having to choose. There are a million different excuses for why your choices were never really your own, and why your mistakes aren't technically mistakes. But sooner or later, the debt must be paid. It's hard to get it out of your head.

It's only at night, right as you fall asleep, that you can finally feel the burden lift off your shoulders. Dreams come and go without a second thought. Your sleeping mind has no choice but to own itself, to forgive itself, to forget itself. Yet your body doesn't quite trust its own judgment, and keeps your limbs locked and frozen in place. So even then, at a time when you're free to do as you please, you're still the only thing that's holding you back.

There will always be a certain lingering question you keep asking about yourself, that never really goes away: to what degree are you responsible? Any clear and unambiguous answer is surely doomed to be a fantasy. So you might as well learn to live with the mystery. Forgive yourself or hold yourself accountable. Try to be yourself or try to be better. Let go or don't let go. Whatever helps you sleep at night.

From *wither*, to become weak and shriveled + *whither*, to what place + *will*, the ability to make choices.

winnewaw

n. an unexpected burst of good news that only makes you skeptical, believing that every sudden rise in your fortunes must inevitably be accompanied by an impending fall, which leaves you feeling uneasy at the end of a really good day, waiting around for the punch line.

Middle English *winne*, joy + *wawe*, woe. Compare *williwaw*, a sudden blast of wind descending from the mountains to the sea. Pronounced "*win*-uh-waw."

ironsick

adj. feeling hollowed out by excessive exposure to modern technology, which is so fast and stimulating that it makes everything else feel drab and messy by comparison—as if you'd unwittingly developed a psychological allergy to chaos, which leaves you feeling punchy and lonely and numb, even though your life might be as peaceful and predictable as it's ever been.

From *iron sick*, a nautical term for when an old ship's iron nails become rusted out, allowing seepage of seawater through the wooden hull.

nemotia

n. the fear that you're utterly powerless to change the world around you, looking on helplessly at so many intractable problems out there—slums that sprawl from horizon to horizon, daily headlines of an unstoppable civil war, a slick of air pollution blanketing the skyline—which makes the act of trying to live your own life feel grotesque and self-indulgent, as if you're rubbernecking through the world.

Slovenian *nemočen*, powerless. Pronounced "nih-*moh*-shah."

wollah

n. something you've misunderstood for years without knowing it—a familiar word with a weird pronunciation, a favorite saying that means the opposite of what you thought, a well-known factoid that was disproven years ago while you weren't looking—making you want to stress-test the foundations of your understanding of reality.

A mispronunciation of the French *voilà*, "behold!" Pronounced "*wawl*-uh."

grayshift

n. the tendency for future goals and benchmarks to feel huge when viewed in advance, only to fade into banality as soon as you've achieved them—finally reaching the top of the ladder, only to notice it circling back around like a hamster wheel.

A variation on *redshift* and *blueshift*, the astronomical processes that make objects moving away look redder than they really are, and objects moving toward you look bluer.

achenia

n. the maddening sense that the world is too complex to even begin to understand, that whenever you try to answer even the most trivial question, it quickly tangles into a thicket of complications and melts into a quicksand of nuance, leaving you flailing for something solid to hold on to, struggling to come up with anything you could say that is definitively 100 percent true.

From *achene*, the fruit that contains the seed of a flowering plant, which is often confused for the seed itself. Whenever you think you've arrived at the heart of something, it only ends up hidden away inside some other more complicated structure. Pronounced "uh-*kee*-nee-uh."

moriturism

n. a tiny jolt of awareness that someday you will die, which leaves you lying awake in bed whispering silently to yourself, *Oh, right, this is it*; an unsettling reminder that your life is not just a game you're playing or a story you'll be telling later, but your one and only glimpse of what the universe has to offer, like a kid waking up in the back seat of the family car at night, having just pulled into a bright neon gas station, looking around for a moment or two, before settling back in for the long road trip, sleeping for miles and miles off into the dark.

Latin *morituri*, "we who are about to die." Pronounced "moh-*rich*-uh-riz-uhm.

furosha

n. the eerie tranquility of fast-moving clouds, who pass through your patch of sky like a drifter stepping into your entryway to warm up for a minute, ruffling the ice from his beard before he nods his gratitude and turns back into the air.

Japanese ふ浪者 (*furōsha*), vagrant, vagabond. Onomatopoeic to the sound of a sudden gust of wind. Pronounced "fuh-*roh*-shuh."

LACHESISM

longing for the clarity of disaster

For a million years, we've watched the sky and huddled in fear. Feeling the thunder rumble deep in our chests, peering up at the storm clouds gathering on the horizon like an army preparing to invade. Even if you try filling the room with TV weather warnings to give yourself a sense of control, you can still taste the chaos hanging in the air.

And yet, somewhere deep down, you find yourself rooting for the storm, hoping for the worst. As if a part of you is tired of waiting, wondering when the world will fall apart—by lot, by fate, by the will of the gods. Almost daring them to grant your wish. But really, you can wish all you want, because life is a game of chance. And each passing day is another flip of the coin.

You can't help but take this life for granted. Your eyes gradually adjust to the color of the walls, and your ears tune out the chatter. And while your brain goes numb trying to shake off your complacency, your heart can't sit still, and your gut is hungry for chaos. Itching to get struck by lightning, plunge over a waterfall, or survive a plane crash. Hoping the trauma will somehow change you, leaving you hardened, stripped down, with clear eyes and a clear mission, forced to choose the one thing worth saving while everything else burns to ash, or send one final message to the people you love the most. Longing to watch society break down one pillar after the next, so you can find out what's truly important, and let everything else fall away.

The apocalypse is one of the oldest fantasies we have. But it's not about skipping to the end of the story. It's a longing for *revelation*, a revealing of what we already know but cannot see—that none of this is guaranteed, and there's no such thing as "ordinary life." That our civilization is just an agreement, one that could be revoked at any time. That beneath our rules and quarrels, we're stuck together on a wide-open planet where anything can happen, which leaves us no choice but to survive, to build a shelter, and find each other in the storm. Knowing that every passing day is very nearly miraculous, a cascading series of accidents that just happens to fall our way.

Eventually, the storm will pass, the skies will clear, and we'll pick up our lives just where we left them, no more urgently than before. We'll soak in the sunshine as if none of it mattered, forgetting the sense of fellowship we once found in the shelter.

That's alright. It's just life—it's not the end of the world.

In Ancient Greek mythology, Lachesis is the middle of the three Fates, the one who decides how much time is to be allotted to each of us, measuring out the thread of life with her rod. Pronounced "*lahk*-uh-siz-uhm."

arroia

n. the wish that you could've enjoyed a dry run of your life—muddling through once quickly, then going back to do it all over again, this time for real.

Spanish *arroyo*, a dried-up streambed waiting for a storm, literally a "dry run." Pronounced "uh-*roi*-uh."

knellish

adj. afraid to relax your body and drift off to sleep because you can't help but notice how much it rhymes with death—lying flat on your back, your hands clumped on your chest, trying to force yourself to let go of consciousness, knowing you'll almost certainly find your grip again but unsure exactly how that happens.

Armenian քնել (*k'nel*), sleep + *knell*, a ringing announcement of a death. Pronounced "*nel*-ish."

angosis

n. the malaise that results from having unlimited access to something, which only seems to drain away its value—a cheat code that ruins the game, a camera that holds a million random snapshots, or having so much free time that all your goals dissolve in it.

Maori *ango*, open + Latin *angō*, I cause pain or distress. Pronounced "ang-*goh*-sis."

mogging folly

n. the act of deliberately squandering your time, lazing about as if none of this is worth a damn, letting precious hours spool away slowly like the string of a runaway kite.

From *mog*, to enjoy one's self in a quiet, easy, comfortable manner + *folly*, a foolish act.

ecsis

n. the haunting sense of mystery infused into certain random details that beckons you to wonder how it ended up here at this point in time—marveling at a patch of white on a dog's chest, a bubble trapped in an old window, a glimpse of Saturn's rings shivering in a telescope lens— knowing that behind the thing itself is a long chain of causes and effects that veers off into the shadows of pre-history, anchored somewhere near the dawn of time, even though the end result is somehow *right there in front of you*, shimmering in place.

Indonesian *eksis*, to exist, to be. Pronounced "*ek*-sis."

Fig. 16. Chthosis. | Collage by John Koenig | dictionaryofobscuresorrows.com

CHTHOSIS

the awareness of how little we really know

There's something unsettling about the idea of a black hole. To think that there's a threshold beyond which there is no return, with everything that crosses it locked away forever, a treasure box of mysteries that can never be opened. But then again, most of life is like that. You are surrounded by event horizons wherever you go. You can sense it in the black void at the foot of the basement stairs, or while driving in a ghostly fog that seems to erase the world beyond your windshield, or when treading water in the ocean, feeling miles of heavy nothing below your kicking feet.

There's a certain thrill to those moments, when you dangle yourself over the edge of the abyss, wondering what might be out there. Knowing it might be seething with powerful forces you're unable to see, lurking right there in front of you. But before long, you turn back to the comfortable world you know—the world of streetlamps and door locks, and the lulling chatter of a TV left on in the other room.

The trouble is, you don't know what you don't know. So even when you think you've pulled back from the edge of the abyss, you might've wandered a few steps closer. Of course, you'd just as well prefer not to think about all those unknown unknowns. Every year, there are tens of thousands of people who simply vanish without a trace and are never found. It happens all the time. The owner of a little antiques shop in Wales leaves a note on the door saying, "Back in two minutes," steps down the street to buy an apple and a banana, and is never seen again. The prime minister of Australia goes out for a swim before lunch on a Sunday, and soon enough a new election is held, and the search party is called off for good. An airliner full of passengers settles into its flight path and then disappears from the radar, as if it had never existed.

You don't particularly care to know the proportion of murders that go unsolved for lack of leads, or how easily locks can be picked and systems can be hacked. Surely someone must've tested the integrity of the bridge under your feet, the roof over your head, the medicine you take, the water you drink every day. Surely someone would pass by and help you dig your way out of a snowbank, or notice that your boat still hasn't returned by nightfall, having drifted well out of sight of land. Surely there's some adult somewhere, keeping an eye on things.

But if we're the adults, and there's nobody else to watch out for us, it means we're out here on our own, floating free. And no matter where you go, and no matter how safe you feel, you're still treading water in the deep end, kicking away, vulnerable to forces you can't control. Even now, the ocean of tomorrow is looming just outside your eyeline.

Maybe it's healthy to soak in that feeling, to lean out over the edge and stare into the abyss, and remind ourselves of the weight of everything we don't know. If only to get us to hold on tighter to the structures we do have—the handrail on the basement stairs, the fence around the playground, the rules and norms of a civil society. If we forgo the comfort of absolute certainty, we might be better adults for each other, asking more questions, wondering what we might be missing.

Maybe then we'd feel a little more at home in this mostly unknowable universe, making our peace with the chaos of it, even finding comfort in the responsibility it gives us. *What might be out there? Nobody knows!*

From *chthonic*, dwelling beneath the surface of the Earth. Pronounced "*kthoh*-sis."

nilous

adj. anxious to imagine how many times you must've barely avoided catastrophe—the morning you missed the bus that later went on to crash, the day you stayed onshore when it was a bit too rough out there—which makes it feel like something of a fluke that you've survived this long, as if you're on an unbroken streak of coin flips, heads after heads after heads, wondering when your luck is going to run out.

Old English *nigh*, almost + *nihil,* nothing. Pronounced "*nahy*-lis."

offtides

adj. beginning to suspect that you're living in a bizarre alternate reality, as if you had stumbled into a shimmering "What if?" thought bubble that somehow kept going, episode after episode.

After *off*, the state of being not quite normal or sane + *offsides*, a sports offense in which you find yourself on the wrong side at the wrong moment + *tides*, the normal ebb and flow of time.

starlorn

n. a sense of loneliness looking up at the night sky, feeling like a castaway marooned in the middle of the ocean, whose currents are steadily carrying off all other castaways— entire worlds and stars whose only remnant is a scrap of light they flung overboard centuries ago, a message in a bottle that's only just now washing up on our shores.

From *star*, a luminous dot in the cloudless sky + *-lorn*, sorely missing. Pronounced "*stahr*-lawrn."

caucic

adj. afraid that the rest of your life is already laid out in front of you, that you're being swept inexorably along a series of predictable milestones—from school to graduation to career to marriage to kids to retirement to death—which makes you wish you could pull off to the side of the road for a little while, to stretch your legs and spread out the map so you can double-check that you're headed the right way.

Middle English *cauci*, path or road + *caustic*, able to burn or corrode living tissue. Pronounced "*kaw*-sik."

irrition

n. regret at having cracked the code of something, which leaves you wishing you could forget the pattern—longing to unsee an optical illusion, to unlearn the formula behind your favorite songs and shows and movies, or re-canonize a role model you made the mistake of meeting in person.

Tahitian *iriti*, to translate + *iriti*, to be convulsed. Pronounced "ih-*ri*-shun."

eftless

adj. mildly disappointed that you'll never be able to attend your own memorial service; frustrated that you could spend your entire life trying to build some sort of legacy to leave behind, but just barely miss your chance to catch a glimpse of what that legacy might be.

German *Effekt*, effect + *less*. As he was dying at age forty, Franz Kafka instructed his friend Max Brod to burn all his literary works upon his death, but Brod famously defied the request and published them to worldwide acclaim. At the time, Max Brod had been a household name, a celebrated author whose first novel was hailed as a masterpiece. Meanwhile, Kafka had spent his life walking the streets of Prague as a complete unknown, and died without ever suspecting that his hometown would soon become synonymous with his name. The world had been unequivocal in its judgment of the two writers, but posterity soon overturned the verdict.

beloiter

v. intr. to look around in a state of mild astonishment that your life is somehow *still going*, as if a part of you had just assumed that your allotment of days would've been used up by now, standing there like a player at a slot machine, perpetually surprised that your winnings continue to trickle out, but not sure what you're supposed to do now.

From *to be* + *to loiter*, to hang around someplace with no particular agenda. Pronounced "bih-*loi*-ter."

karanoia

n. the terror of the blank page, which can feel both liberating and confining, in both the limitlessness of its potential and the looseness of its boundaries.

Japanese 空の (*kara-no*), blank. Pronounced "kar-uh-*noi*-uh."

YRÁTH

hunger for mystery
in a time of easy answers

We'll never invent a computer that could give us an answer to the meaning of life, the universe, and everything. But you have to wonder how close we might come one day—how many intractable mysteries will end up being solvable, how many inconveniences will get fixed over time.

It's not hard to imagine how satisfying it would feel, cruising through the world on autopilot, along the optimum route at the optimum speed, hitting only the top-rated destinations. To have every question answered, every obstacle avoided, every risk insured in real time, with your odds of failure already calculated to the third decimal place, leaving you with little else to do but listen to a serene digital voice chime in with reminders and progress reports, muttering to yourself, *I know, I know, I know.*

But what are the odds that even then, you'd only end up feeling lost? Because there's a part of you that doesn't particularly want easy answers. That bristles at spoilers and step-by-step instructions, that wants to be fooled by magic tricks, that stirs to life whenever your phone dies and you find yourself lost in neighborhoods you'd otherwise never get to see. There's still the art of the slow unveiling—learning

the world by heart, piece by piece, in no particular rush—
allowing yourself to soak in the mystery of things.

There's some beauty left in mystery. The beauty of knowing that the ocean is still mostly uncharted, inhabited by
creatures nobody's ever seen, except for the scars they leave
on the faces of whales. The beauty that we have names for
planets that we're not even sure exist. That the people of Ancient Greece lived out their lives within walking distance of
Mount Olympus but never felt compelled to climb it, opting
instead to let their gods live out their immortal lives in peace.

We should count ourselves lucky that we were born so
early in history—back when the machine was only just starting to boot up, when it was still possible to go outside and
savor a moment of in-betweenness. When you could still get
out there in the early morning, pulling a canoe through the
reeds on the edge of the lake, dropping a line, and waiting for
a nibble in silence.

If nothing else, that silence reminds you to pay attention
to the nature of things. Calibrating your senses, learning to
recognize a glimmer of something real, turning in the deep.
You have no idea what's going to happen, if anything happens
at all—but that's alright, you've got nowhere to be.

As of this writing, there's still no computer that can give
us all the answers. No fish finder that can tell you when to
set the hook. So you might as well sit back and soak in the
suspense, and thank the gods that it's still possible to get lost
in the middle of nowhere, watching your line scribble across

the water, humming softly to yourself, *I don't know, I don't know, I don't know.*

Origin unknown. Pronounced "ee-*rawth*."

nodrophobia

n. the fear of irrevocable actions and irreversible processes—knowing that a colorful shirt will fade a little more with every wash, that your tooth enamel is wearing away molecule by molecule, never to grow back.

Greek μονόδρομος (*monódromos*), one-way street + -φοβία (-*phobía*), fear. Pronounced "noh-droh-*foh*-bee-uh."

evertheless

n. the fear that this is ultimately as good as your life is ever going to get—that the ebb and flow of your fortunes is actually just now hitting its high-water mark, and soon enough you'll sense the tide of life slowly begin to recede.

From *ever* + *nevertheless*. Pronounced "ev-er-thuh-*les*."

tornomov

n. the weird hollowness of trying to imagine the distant future—struggling to place it in any sort of context you'd find relatable but straining to believe it could feel all that different from the world around you.

A word that looks like *tomorrow* from a distance but is actually something else that you can't really explain. Occasionally nuclear engineers try to work out how to warn future generations to stay away from radioactive waste sites, where it won't be safe to dig for ten thousand years. There are many challenges: stainless steel signs will eventually rust away, etchings in granite will be buffed clean by sandstorms, huge menacing earthworks shrouded in vegetation. Any words or symbols we leave behind will surely have lost their meaning by then, the Gregorian calendar replaced five times over, erasing any sense of when AD 12000 was supposed to be. It makes you wonder: If it seems impossible to pass a message beyond our own little neighborhood in time, impossible even to warn our descendants not to dig into poisoned ground, what relationship do we have to them? Pronounced "*tohr*-noh-mawf."

aponemia

n. the peculiar quality of never having chosen to be born, which is shared by everyone else around you; the curious awareness that even though earthly life might be the most exciting party in the universe, somehow everyone in attendance had been dragged here by a friend or stumbled in by accident.

Greek απονέμω (*aponémo*), to bestow. Pronounced "ap-uh-*nee*-mee-uh."

rialtoscuro

n. the disorientation of stepping outside a movie theater into unexpected darkness—a twinge of jet lag after letting your mind escape to some other world for a while, only to be thrown abruptly back into reality.

Italian *rialto*, a theater district + *oscuro*, dark, obscure. Compare *chiaroscuro*, which describes a quality of visual art that emphasizes the contrast between deep shade and bright light. Pronounced "ree-al-toh-*skyoor*-oh."

adomania

n. the sense that the future is arriving ahead of schedule, that all those years with fanciful names are bursting from their hypothetical cages into the arena of the present, furiously bucking your grip while you slip around in your saddle, with one hand reaching for the reins, the other waving up high like a schoolkid who finally knows the answer to the question.

Italian *a domani*, until tomorrow + *mania*. Pronounced "ad-uh-*mey*-nee-uh."

Fig. 17. Tiris. | Collage by John Koenig | dictionaryofobscuresorrows.com

TIRIS

the bittersweet awareness that all things must end

Even right at the start of things, you can feel the sense of an ending. The way you're still only settling into vacation while mentally preboarding your flight home, or how soon after starting a new relationship you start to wonder exactly how this one ends. Even before you've purchased the carton of milk in your hands, you're already turning it over, looking for the expiration date.

In the end, all goods are perishable. Everything is transient. Look down at your wedding ring and you can already see it shining on your granddaughter's hand, knowing she'll occasionally spin it around her finger when she gets nervous. Fill up a journal or frame a family photo, and you can already feel it sitting in a box on the shelf of an antique shop.

So it goes, and such is life, and this too shall pass. *Anicca* and *anitya, mono no aware, sic transit gloria mundi, amen.* But back when you were a kid, you couldn't help but look at the world like a still life painting, pretty and static and hopelessly boring. If you were lucky, there were people around you who tried to insulate you from change, who were there to reassure you, "Don't you worry, I'm not going anywhere. Not for a long time."

As a result, you couldn't help but feel shocked when things started disappearing without warning—your best friend moved away, the video store closed, the family dog grew old and died. That incipient sense of loss is what drew you closer to those still alive and well, and gave you a reason to pay closer attention, hoarding details like a honeybee rushing from flower to flower, because you knew summer wouldn't last forever.

Eventually with the benefit of years, you began to notice shifts too subtle to register from one day to the next. How quickly a bouquet starts to wilt, how a fringe of white sweeps over your father's hair. You keep reminding yourself to make peace with the churn. But for some reason you still find yourself shocked when things change in ways you didn't see coming, as if you keep falling for the same old sleight of hand.

Of course, sometimes you have to thank the gods that nothing lasts forever. It's a relief to know that your mistakes will start to fade as soon as they hit the page, that when the harvest fails, a new spring is already on its way. We don't have to wait long for another shot at redemption.

Other times, the impermanence of everything around us feels haunting. To think that a thousand-year-old cathedral won't always be there. That entire cities can be forgotten in a manner of decades, vibrant languages dwindled into obscurity, fearsome gods relinquished to old books, old books turned to dust. How casually the world discards our work, with nothing but a shrug. There's even an odd comfort in hearing how long it takes for Styrofoam to decompose—all the better for humans to have left some sort of mark on this world, as if each discarded coffee cup is just another way of saying, *We were here*.

You begin to wonder: Why bother making long-term plans? What's the point of getting invested, when the sitcom will only get canceled, the house will break apart, the sand mandala swept into the trash? Why let yourself fall in love with someone when the best-case scenario is you'll end up losing them?

This question has persisted for centuries, appearing in so many songs and poems and conversations by those who came before us. Some of their tombstones are still around today, for a little while longer at least. It'll be a while before the rain wears away the granite. The mountains too are steadily crumbling away, inch by inch, year by year, soon to be recycled back into the fiery mantle from which they came. Alas, even the world is not long for this world, soon to be swallowed up by the sun. Soon enough the stars will burn out, too, leaving little else but an echo of radiation, reverberating in a heatless void. And there will be no way to tell that time is passing at all.

There's a certain kinship there, shared by all things. The stars and the tombstones, the family dog and the honeybees. A comfort to think that we are all united in our impermanence. Because if even the mountains have lifetimes, and our own galaxy will one day be no more, then there's no solid definition of what permanence even means. *Eternity, infinity, forever:* these are nonsense words, poetical abstractions, useful only to spice up mathematicians' thought experiments. The finiteness of reality takes it out of the hands of the gods and gives us control. Without an objective yardstick to establish what eternity looks like, it's up to us to define what timeframe we view as normal, and calibrate our own understanding of what *fleeting* and *lasting* really mean.

You can take a summer afternoon playing yard games with your family and make it last for years. Spend an eternity sitting by the fire with your loved ones, or tell a bedtime story to your kids that they'll remember for eons. Grow a garden, and revel in its sweetness for a little while, before it all withers away, buried in snow and ash. Drop by to visit with friends, chatting about nothing particularly important. Call your parents. Go out and look at the stars while they're still visible. Doodle away in the margins, and make art for its own sake, even though you know it won't last more than a few thousand years. You can sit in a chair listening to music, while music still exists; you can curl up and read a good book while the language is still alive, while the words still have meaning.

The meaning of things isn't an emergent property of how long they last. We are the ones who define them for ourselves, if only for our own satisfaction. It is an honor reserved for mortals; we just have to have the courage to do it. To decide for ourselves which fleeting, precious, interminable moments we'll carry with us right to the end. Maybe to the mountains, they won't amount to all that much. But to the honeybees, it's more than enough.

To the honeybees, summer never ends. They live for a few months at most, barely long enough to feel the seasons change. They have no need to remind each other to put themselves out there, gathering their rosebuds while they may. You can hear them buzzing deep in their hives, trading bits of sweetness they've gathered out in the world. How easily they pass the nectar back and forth between their bodies, freely mixing it all together as if none of it made a difference, knowing they'll never live long enough to taste it all.

And yet, their honey is the one thing that never expires, that never loses its sweetness. Maybe that buzzing sound is just another way of saying, *We are here.*

From *Tír na nÓg*, the land of everlasting youth in Irish folklore + *hubris*, excessive pride or arrogance, especially toward a god. "Our songs will all be silenced," said Orson Welles, "but what of it? Go on singing." Pronounced "*teer*-uhs."

AFTER WORDS

NEOLOGISTICS

In the twelve or so years since I began writing this dictionary, the most frequently asked question I've received is this: "Are these words real, or are they made up?"

At first the answer seemed obvious. Nope, not real. I made them all up. But about halfway through this project, something strange happened. Late one night, I wrote a definition called *sonder*—the awareness that everyone around you is the main character of their own story—and posted it to my website, dictionaryofobscuresorrows.com. In the original definition I compared each stranger's life to an anthill, that looks so simple on the surface but is actually an entire universe sprawling deep underground, with elaborate passageways to thousands of other lives that you'll never know existed.

Within minutes I started getting emails from readers saying, "Thank you for giving voice to something I've felt all my life." I was astonished by how universal this feeling seemed to be, though I'd only ever felt it in glimmers of solitude, letting my mind wander while glancing over at the other cars passing on the highway, wondering where they might be going. How fitting that this definition gave me a glimpse into the lives of thousands of strangers I would never otherwise have a chance to meet, hidden away in the far corners of the world. Not long after, I began to notice *sonder* being used earnestly online. And then I started seeing it in the real world, appearing in coffee shops and tattoos and galleries and symphonies, even overhearing it in real-life conversations taking place next to me. Really, there's no stranger feeling than making up a word only to watch it take on a life of its own.

It made me go back and rethink the question. Really, who am I to say which words are real and which aren't? Sure, *sonder* wasn't real when I wrote it, but one day it might catch on, graduating to another more prestigious dictionary, taking its place alongside *robot*, *nerd*, *dreamscape*, and *serendipity*, each of which rose up through the ranks in exactly the same way. It felt empowering to imagine that so many of the words we use every day were coined by people not too different from me.

So I switched up my answer, and started to tell people, "It's up to you. A word is only real if you want it to be." Maybe words are like those dirt paths that cut diagonally across the lawns of college campuses. When the proper path is too difficult or ineffective to express an idea—when "self-portrait with a phone" doesn't seem to cover it anymore—someone will cut to the chase and blaze a new trail. And when others see it they'll follow, and soon enough the shortcut becomes the main road, because a critical mass of people wanted it to be there.

Of course, that implies it's just a question of numbers. So then, how many people have to know a word before we can say that it's real? Perhaps we should think of language as a tool of inception, as if we're scanning a drawer full of keys, wondering which one will open the most doors into other people's heads. If a word gets you into one or two brains, it's not really worth knowing, but a million brains is a different story. Clearly, a real word is one that gives you access to as many brains as possible.

This idea got me thinking. By that measure, the realest word of all must be this one:

According to linguists, that is the most commonly understood word in the world, the closest thing we have to a master key. The only problem with that is, well, nobody seems to know what those two letters are supposed to stand for. "Orl Korrect"? "Old Kinderhook"? Or perhaps it was borrowed from one of a dozen other languages around the world, any of which could make a plausible claim to the origins of the term. Nobody knows for sure, and we may never know. But somehow it doesn't matter. And the fact that it doesn't matter says something fundamental about how we use language.

For a dictionary, the parable of *okay* is a reminder to stay humble. To be sure, words are enormously powerful; they give meaning to everything they touch. But a word on its own can't give meaning to itself. It doesn't matter what its origins were, how long it's been out there, or how many people know it. Context is everything. Perhaps the only thing. In language, as in life, meaning isn't something that's built in. It emerges spontaneously in the interactions between elements, even those that are meaningless on their own—a single word, a single moment, a single life. String a handful of notes into a song, and anyone who hears it can be moved to tears, or break out dancing. But a note by itself means nothing at all.

Finally, here was a satisfying answer. Yes, my words are made up—but then, all words are made up. Every single one. That's part of their magic.

As much as we all tend to take them very seriously, words are just patterns in the air, a figurative shorthand, no more real than the constellations in the sky. Really, that's all a word is: a constellation of thoughts and feelings that our ancestors traced into memorable shapes. Many are crude and exaggerated, bearing little resemblance to the things they're supposed to represent. Certain other cultures might connect the dots very differently, sometimes overlapping, sometimes untranslatable. And they all tend to warp and drift over time, falling out of date or taking on new meanings. Still, they remain a calming presence in our lives, seemingly fixed in place, something we can turn to whenever we're feeling lost.

It's no wonder that words seem so utterly real to us, because we so desperately want them to be. Whenever life feels chaotic and uncertain and everything runs together, words offer us a sense of clarity and definition, with clean lines that separate one thing from another. You may not know who you are or what will happen tomorrow, but at least you know the difference between *magma* and *lava*, a *strait* and a *fjord*, a *thrush* and a *shrike*. Just the act of putting something into words can give you the impression that everything is under control.

Such is the blessing and the curse of language. Words are so effective at simplifying reality that it's easy to lose track of how much detail is being left out. Of course you know the world is far more complex and ambiguous than it seems on paper. But if you're not paying attention, language can sweep through your mind like a virus, breaking everything down into neat categories and easily definable terms. You find yourself sizing up your life in reference to airy abstractions, rather than the reality on the ground. Sure, your relationship feels intimate, but is it *love*? Your work is interesting, but is it *art*? You've lived here for ten years, but are you *home*? You've got a lot going on in your life, but are you *happy*? Are you a *success*?

More than anything else, that's what my years of making up words has taught me. It altered my perspective of language, highlighting how easy it is to give words more weight than they deserve. It's as if we've become so fixated on the constellations that we're unable to see the stars.

Sometimes I wonder if the dictionary itself should never have been invented in the first place, because it gives us a misleading impression of what gives words their meaning, and how stable that meaning really is. By conveying an artificial sense of consensus, dictionaries make it all too easy to believe that our words define us, instead of the other way around.

Lately I've even started to wonder if we're approaching a tipping point, where the world we talk about feels more real than the world we live in. Call it a state of *hyperdefinition*, when we become so preoccupied with making reality fit into definitions that we lose sight of what the reality is. If you try too aggressively to sort everything into categories, the details of things don't really matter. As a result, nothing feels unique. Everyone you meet fits into a handful of predictable types; every relationship becomes a kind of game; every work of art becomes a commentary on genre; every discussion of values devolves into squabbles over semantics. It makes everyday life feel faintly hypothetical, infused with irony, like you're living inside a political cartoon.

Still, there are those rare moments when you manage to tune out the chatter in your head, look around, and remind yourself of the meaning of things. In this book I called this feeling *ambedo*, a trance of emotional clarity, a moment you experience for its own sake. It was one of the hardest definitions to pin down, because it tends to hover right at the edge of your awareness: the sense that *this isn't it*, that there's another dimension hidden just beneath the surface of everything around you. For a moment you're able to shake off the spell of language and see things as they are, in all their unknowable complexity. This world is far bigger than the handful of places you've seen or heard about; your inner experience is far richer than the stories you tell yourself; your loved ones are far deeper than the roles they play in your life; strangers are more than just extras to fill out the background. No matter how deep you sink your teeth into things, you're only ever scratching the surface. Despite what dictionaries would have us believe, this world is still mostly undefined.

If only we could find a way to hold on to this awareness, and remind ourselves that we're not done yet. Luckily, that's what words are good for—they give meaning to everything they touch. We have the power to use them as we will, even if it means starting over, wiping the slate clean so we can get to work redefining the world around us, until our language more closely matches the reality we experience.

I think that's the reason why I wanted this book to exist, why I spent so many years chasing this obsession, and why it's brought me so much joy over that time. I don't know much about anything, and I can't back this up with any hard data, but I wholeheartedly recommend the practice of inventing new words to pin down whatever it is you're feeling. It loosens your mental frameworks and gives you a sense of ownership over the stories you tell yourself.

Now is the time to go looking for gaps in the lexicon, scribbling monsters in the blank spaces of the map, to alert others that *something* might be down there. And if you invent a word and it feels like nonsense, all the better. We could all use a little more nonsense, if only to remind us not to get too caught up in the models we've imposed on the world. Language is not reality. The map is not the territory. As Alan Watts liked to say, "The menu is not the meal."

That's my answer, when all is said and done: make your words real, even if you have to make them up as you go. If you have the courage to define yourself, and take ownership over the terms by which you live your life, something mysterious will happen: the walls will fall away, and the world will open up.

A word is like the thread that leads out of the labyrinth. It's not much—it's so thin it's barely there—but it's enough to remind you of things you already know, so you can retrace your steps when you're lost in the dark. To leap into the depths is a kind of joy. To chase an impossible dream is a joy. To feel anything at all is a joy.

ON GRATITUDE

For some reason, I find it a much easier task to define grief than to express gratitude, though the two emotions feel so similar they might well be synonyms, or two sides of the same coin—you can't mourn something you've lost without celebrating the rarity of its presence in your life. Still, it would take a whole other book to convey the gratitude I feel when I look back on this project.

There is so much I could say to my wife, Anna, my backboard and backer, and daughter, Charlotte, who kept my heart beating even before she was born. To my teachers and mentors, especially Robert Bly, who inspired me to begin writing, and Alex Lemon, who inspired me to continue. To my wise and patient editors Jonathan Cox and Zachary Knoll, and literary agents Heather Karpas and Kristyn Keene Benton, along with all the others who worked behind the scenes to make this book a reality. To each of my illustrators, whose work is the definition of silence, and to all the unsung contributors to the commons, from Wikipedia and Wiktionary to Onelook and the dozens of dictionaries I've plundered for raw material. To my family and friends, and the world-famous creatives I'm proud to call my colleagues. And to my writers' group back in college, the Future Failures, I hereby present this week's submission. Be gentle.

But most of all, I have no words to express my gratitude to the many readers who have sent me notes and comments over the years, offering their support for this project, describing feelings that haunted them, or giving me a glimpse of their own story, hoping I could invent a word that would help them make sense of it all.

There was the young woman in Pakistan who would observe her ninety-six-year-old grandfather across the dinner table every night, mystified by the enormity of his life experience, so different from her own. There was a deployed U.S. Marine who secretly dreaded video chatting with people back home, because it made him feel never closer but never farther away. A psychologist in Chile who wondered why her friends only engaged with her when she asked them questions, but showed little curiosity about her own inner life. The doctor in India who wondered if he had lost his youth chasing the career his parents wanted for him, yet still found meaning in the intimate glimpses he gets into patients' family lives. The son of Holocaust survivors who retreated to the mountains to find peace, but found the silence unnerving. A woman in South Africa who didn't know how to reassure her grandson that there was goodness in this world, when she couldn't convince herself.

So much longing, so many missed connections and haunting memories. So many desperate attempts to control how they felt about certain people, wishing they could turn off their love, or turn it back on again.

It's been an otherworldly experience, reading these glimpses into strangers' lives at random points in my day. Some days I'd get emails from two people half a world away from each other, describing the same sense of cosmic lostness—but neither had any way of knowing that their voices had accidentally harmonized across the world, converging in my inbox.

Over time I began to get a sense of how much we all must secretly have in common. How many of us must be burdened by the same unanswerable questions, muttering the same thoughts to the steering wheel or the shower wall. And whenever I felt alone, or confused, or like a stranger to myself, I knew I was tapping into an undercurrent of humanity that connected me invisibly with so many others who feel exactly as I do, each in their own lives. That's the magic of expressing how you feel, as precisely as you can. If nothing else, it can serve as a powerful reminder to all of us that we're not alone.

John

A WORD OF ADVICE

ollyollyoxenfree

INDEX

ABOUT THE AUTHOR

JOHN KOENIG lives in Minnesota with his wife and daughter. In 2009, he created *The Dictionary of Obscure Sorrows*, which began as a blog at dictionaryofobscuresorrows.com before expanding into a series on YouTube. His work has been acclaimed by John Green, *New York* magazine, and the guys from *Radiolab*.

He can be reached at obscuresorrows@gmail.com.